Montague

 Need to Read SERIES

D0499419

Great Stories from Real Life

Taken from *Guideposts* Magazine

Tyndale House Publishers, Inc.
WHEATON, ILLINOIS

Cover illustrations copyright © 1990 John Dickenson

Scripture quotations are from *The Simplified Living Bible,* copyright © 1990 by KNT Charitable Trust. All rights reserved. Used by permission.

Adapted for the Need to Read Series from *Best Stories from Guideposts* copyright © 1987 by Guideposts Associates, Inc. Used by permission.

ISBN 0-8423-1171-8
Library of Congress Catalog Card Number 90-71454
Copyright © 1991 by Tyndale House Publishers, Inc.
All rights reserved
Printed in the United States of America

95 94 93 92 91
9   8   7   6   5   4   3   2   1

CONTENTS

READING SCORES
Flesch-Kincaid: 1
Gunning-Fog: 3

OUT OF THE FIRE
by Robert R. Searle, Oakland, California

It was the middle of the night, 3:00 A.M. The Oakland Police got a call. "Someone is breaking into a bar," my partner told me. "Let's go and catch him!"

My partner and I hurried to the scene. It was a good night for us. We caught the guy.

The back-up police took the robber away. I sat down with my partner to write the report.

My partner's name was Frank. Really, he was my teacher. You see, I was a rookie cop. It was my first year. Frank had to teach me what to do. He taught me how to catch burglars — and how to write reports.

Frank was sure of himself. I wasn't. He always knew what to do. I didn't. I enjoyed police work, but sometimes I was afraid. When you're a cop, any mistake you make may be your last.

"Trust yourself," Frank told me. "You will learn. You will know what to do. Trust your gut feelings."

I didn't know if that was right. I had learned to trust God, not myself. But maybe Frank was right. I just didn't know.

As we sat at the bar, I shivered. It was cold outside. It was cold inside, too. Even inside the bar, I could see the clouds of my breath. I told myself, *Next time, wear long johns.*

All of a sudden, we heard a sound from outside. It came from the road. Tires screeched. We heard the crash of metal against metal. Then we heard a smash. It was the sound of metal against wood, and breaking glass.

"What was that?" I shouted.

"Let's take a look," Frank said.

We hurried out into the cold night. We looked down the street. A truck was off to one side. On the other side, a car was smashed against a building. The wooden building was beginning to burn.

We quickly figured out what happened. The truck had run into the car. That was the first crash we heard. Then the car rammed into the building. That was the smash we heard, with breaking glass.

We ran toward the burning car. *Oh, no!* I thought. *What if someone is caught inside the car?*

My gut feeling was telling me to run away. I was afraid of fire. In my dreams, I used to see myself trapped in fire. That scared me.

Still, we kept running toward the car. Frank stopped and pulled out his radio. He called for a fire truck. I kept running. As I got closer to the car, I saw more clearly. The back of the car was not on fire. Not yet.

The gas tank was in the back. If that caught fire, the car would explode.

A man was running toward me. "Hurry! Hurry!" he said. "A woman is trapped inside the car!" That was just what I was afraid of.

I got to the car and looked in. Yes, a woman was trapped under the dashboard. She was out cold. I tried to open the door. It was jammed.

The fire was still in the front of the car. *I might have time to save her,* I thought.

The glass of the car window was broken. I pushed the pieces away. I reached inside. I grabbed the woman's arm. I couldn't move her.

Frank came running up. "Fire trucks are on their way," he said. He saw what I was doing. He ran to the other side of the car. The front door was jammed, but the back door opened.

I kept trying to pull the woman up. Frank got into the back seat. He reached over the seat to help. We still couldn't move her.

The fire was spreading. Now the inside of the car was starting to burn.

"Get out of the car!" Frank shouted. He was my teacher. I was supposed to do what he said. But I didn't want to leave this woman. If I left, she would die in the fire.

"Gas is spilling all over!" Frank shouted again. "Get out of the car!"

I looked at the woman again. I wanted to save her, but I couldn't. That made me very sad. But I had to get out.

I backed away from the car. The fire was spreading through the building. It was spreading over the car. It was like my bad dreams. There was fire all around me. But it was the woman who was trapped in the flames.

"We did all we could," Frank said. He was trying to make me feel better. "We just couldn't save her," he said.

My heart was beating fast. As I looked at the fire, I prayed. "God, I can't do a thing to save her. Can't you save her?"

All of a sudden, a Bible verse came to my mind. Matthew 18:14. "It is not my Father's will that even one of these little ones should die."

The Father is God. I knew that. His "little ones" are everybody — even the woman in the car.

God was telling me something. "I don't want this woman to die," he was saying.

That bothered me. I talked back to God. "God, you aren't telling me to go back into that car. Are you? We tried to save her. We couldn't do it."

My heart almost stopped beating. I was very scared. But I knew I had to go back into that car.

I prayed again. "Lord, you know that I am afraid of fire. You have to make me strong enough to do this."

Before I knew it, I was running to the car. The front door was still jammed. I pulled at the back door. "God, help me get this open," I prayed. I felt that God was close to me.

The door opened. Not very far, but it opened. I could slide sideways into the back seat.

The car was full of smoke. I shouted, "God, show me what to do!" Reaching forward, I touched the woman. I bent forward. I almost fell. The fire was very hot all around me. "God, help me!" I shouted again.

I lifted her up. Her body was very light. It was like someone else was lifting her.

I pushed her legs through the window. Someone outside the car pulled her the rest of the way. She was safe at last. I squeezed through the back door and ran away from the car. Twenty feet away, I turned and looked. Fire was all over the car. I had gotten out just in time.

Frank came up to me. "Bob," he said, "I wanted to help you. But I am afraid of fire."

"So am I," I said.

He looked at me in surprise. "There was just no way we could get her out," he said. "We did the best we could do."

I just smiled. "Frank," I said, "you have always told me to trust myself. This time I trusted God."

READING SCORES:
Flesch-Kincaid: 1
Gunning-Fog: 3

THE DAM BROKE!
by Dave Eby, Toccoa Falls, Georgia

It was raining. It was raining hard! Thunder crashed.
The wind blew against our house. At about 9:30 P.M.,
the lights went out.

The storm had knocked out the power in the whole
area. Some students at Toccoa [tuh-KOH-uh] Falls
College used the darkness to play some pranks. We
lived across the street from the dorm where some
students lived. I am Dean of Men at the college. That
meant I had to deal with these pranks.

It had been a bad day. This did not make it better.

My wife had gone shopping — spending money we
didn't have. The kids had gotten on my nerves at
supper. Then there was the storm. Then the lights went
out. And then the silly pranks.

I went to bed about 12:30. But this night wasn't over.

Up on the mountain above us, a dam had been built.
It was built many years ago. The dam controlled the
flow of water. On one side was a large, man-made
lake. It covered fifty-five acres. It held 176 million
gallons.

On the other side of the dam was Toccoa Falls. This was a lovely waterfall. The water fell 186 feet at this spot. Then it flowed in a gentle river through our town.

On this night, the rain was filling the lake. The wind was shaking the dam. The water ate away at the old dam. All of a sudden, the dam broke. A wall of water burst through. It made a great sound. It was a roar like thunder, only worse.

The 700,000 tons of water raced down the mountain. The water crushed trees as if they were matches. It raced to the waterfall. It fell quickly into the area below.

My wife, Barb, woke up when she heard the sound. So did I. It was 1:30 A.M. At first we thought the earth was shaking. Then Barb knew what had happened. She ran to the window. "The dam broke!" she shouted.

"You're crazy," I said. I ran to the window, too. I looked outside. It took a moment for my eyes to get used to the light. Then I saw — the water had risen. It was nearly up to the windows.

Barb ran to get our children. First she got Kim, our oldest daughter. Kim is seven. Then Barb went to get Kevin, age five, and Kelly, age two. Their bedroom was down the hall.

I tried to break through our window. Then we could climb out. There was a hill beside our house. We could run to higher ground. As I broke through the glass, I cut my arm badly. But I didn't notice. We had put plastic on the windows. I was trying to punch through the plastic. That was a bit like punching Jell-O.

Then the wall of water hit. Barb was in the hallway with the other two kids. Kim was with me in the bedroom.

The house was ripped off the ground. The floor folded up. The walls moved. Then the water began turning the house around. It was like a merry-go-round. Inside the house, we all were thrown around. We grabbed onto any solid thing we could find.

Kim and I were thrown into a side room. The floor pushed up against us. It almost crushed us against the ceiling. Then that room broke off from the rest of the house. We were thrown out into the water.

The roof of the house had come off. It was floating in the water. I grabbed onto it. I helped Kim get on the roof. Then I climbed on, too.

I saw the rest of the house. The water was still turning it around. It floated about fifty yards away. Then it stopped. It was stuck on something.

I thought about Barb and Kevin and Kelly. They were in that house. I thought that they were dead. I tried to tell Kim gently. I said I was afraid the others were lost. She nodded.

But we were still in danger. I saw a small piece of the roof float by us. "Maybe we can get on that," I said. "Then we can paddle over to safe ground." It sounded like a good plan.

"Climb onto my back," I told Kim. She climbed onto my back. Then I jumped.

The small piece of the roof broke. Kim fell off. The water closed over my head. I was sinking.

In the next few moments, I felt all alone. I thought to myself, *My wife is gone. My kids are gone. I am the only one left. No one knows I am here. No one knows how I feel.*

Then, all of a sudden, I felt that God was with me. He was there. That was all I needed. If I died, I would be with God. My family would be there, too.

I felt two small arms grab my neck. "Don't let go of me again, Daddy!" It was Kim's voice. That made me feel strong again.

We were floating on the water again. We hung onto part of a door. "We are still alive," I said. "Maybe Mom and the others are, too!" I began to shout at the top of my lungs. "Barb! Kevin! Kelly!"

I heard a voice across the water. It was Barb. Then I heard Kevin's voice, then Kelly's. We were all happy to be alive. We were also happy that the others were alive.

But we were getting weaker. Barb could not hold Kevin and Kelly much longer. "Pray!" I shouted to her. "Pray that the water will drop!"

Soon we all were praying. We prayed at the top of our lungs. We wanted the others to hear us.

Seconds later, the water began to drop. Soon we could see people on the land. They called to us, "How many are there?"

"All of us!" I shouted. They cheered. We felt a deep peace. God had answered our prayer.

The water dropped even more. We were able to walk onto dry ground. People gave us dry clothes. They gave us warm blankets. They helped me take care of my bleeding arm. We were safe.

But I will never forget that moment under the water. God became real to me in that moment. Now I want to stay close to him.

Let me tell you, I thought life was boring before that flood. Now I see how great it is to be alive. I am glad I can love God every day. I am glad I can serve him.

A man told me, "Remember this. God was with you in that danger. He will also be with you in the boring times."

I know he is. And that makes life less boring.

READING SCORES:
Flesch-Kincaid: 1
Gunning-Fog: 3

JUMP!
by George Rivera, Brooklyn, New York

I was working on my car. A guy I knew came into the garage. He was laughing. "Hey, man," he said. "You should go outside and see the fire."

"What fire?" I asked. I was still working on the car. I didn't even look out from under the hood.

The guy pointed outside. "Down the street!" he said. "One of the tall buildings. One man jumped out a window. Poor guy! He cracked his head on the sidewalk."

I pulled my head out from under the hood. He should not joke about that. "I'm glad you think it's funny," I said.

"Hey, I was just kidding," he said. "No one really jumped. Don't be so uptight."

He walked out of the garage. I bent over the car again. I was upset. He shouldn't joke around like that. It was not right.

But not much was right around here. I should have been at work. I worked for the city of New York. My job was to fix garbage trucks. But sometimes it made me sick. I mean really sick. I could not stand the smell. My doctor told me to get a new job. That was not so easy.

On this day I did not feel well. So I stayed home to work on my own car. And I felt sorry for myself. No one cared about me, I thought. My job made me sick. But I needed the job to make money. And no one cared.

But it could be worse, I thought. *I could be in that burning building.*

I decided to go and see this fire — if there really was a fire. I put my tools away and went outside.

As I walked down the street, I saw people on the corners. Some were drunk. Some were high on drugs. And this was only 10:30 in the morning! This area had gone bad. I had lived here for ten years. I saw it get worse. I used to know the people who lived here. But now they were all strangers. No one cared.

I thought about the fight that happened near here. My brother, Jose (ho-ZAY) was in it. It was a silly fight. But Jose was stabbed to death.

That hurt me very much. Jose had been very close to me. We hung around with each other all the time. He even made sure I went to church. But now he was gone. And no one cared.

I turned the corner and I saw the fire. A four-story building was full of smoke. A crowd of people stood in the street. They were talking and shouting. Some were pointing and waving at the building. Some were crying.

I ran to the scene. Then I looked up. There were two little girls on the top floor. "Help! Help!" they cried.

I felt as if they were my own kids. They just had to get out.

"Has anyone called for fire trucks?" I asked.

"Yes," someone said. "They should be here in five minutes."

That would be too late. I tried to run into the building. The heat was too strong. I had to come back out.

Some boys had found a ladder. But that was too short. It did not even reach the second floor. Something had to be done fast.

I called up to the girls, "Jump! I will catch you!" They did not see me.

"Jump!" I said again. "I will catch you!"

Someone else was behind me. "You are crazy, man," he said. "That is a forty-foot drop. If they land on you, they will kill you! Wait for the fire trucks!"

"You could kill them, too," said someone else. "If you miss them or drop them, they'll die. Don't be a fool!"

I had to admit I was not a large man. I was five-foot-four, a hundred pounds. But there was no choice. Something had to be done. There was no time to waste. "Jump!" I yelled. "Jump!"

The smoke was thick. I could hardly see the girls. And they could hardly see me. "God," I prayed, "help them. Give those girls the courage to jump. Help me catch them, God. Send them straight into my arms. Make me strong enough to catch them."

All of a sudden, I saw one of the girls falling toward me. I held out my arms. With a thud, she landed against my arms and chest. I fell back a little. But I held on with all my might. Then we both fell to the sidewalk. I got up and handed her to someone else. She did not seem to be hurt.

"Are you all right?" I asked. In tears, she nodded.

I looked up at the window for the other girl. The smoke was even thicker. I could not see her at all. I prayed again, "God, don't let me miss her. Guide her into my arms."

Something told me to move back a couple of feet. "Now, you—jump!" I called. "I caught your sister! Do not be afraid!"

The girl stood still on the ledge of the building. She was crying. She was looking through the smoke. Then she jumped.

She fell right into my arms. She was a little bigger than her sister. So she made me fall backwards. But I held on tight. She was all right.

People helped us up. They were all talking at once. "Are you all right? Are you all right?" The two girls were in each other's arms. They were crying, but glad that they were safe. Flash bulbs went off. People were taking our picture. And then the fire trucks came.

Inside of me, I felt calm. For the first time in my life, I knew that God was with me.

The doctors checked us. We were not hurt. One girl had a small scratch on her cheek. But there were no big cuts or bruises.

Later I learned a Bible verse. It said that God keeps his children safe. It says that we can rest on his strong arms (Deuteronomy 33:27). Now I know how I caught those girls. Under my arms were God's arms. He was keeping all three of us safe.

Since then, things have changed for me. I am not so mad about things at work. I am not mad about changes in my area. I feel better. I don't get sick so much. I am planning to go back to school.

Each day I try to do my best. And I know God is holding me up. He cares.

READING SCORES:
Flesch-Kincaid: 1
Gunning-Fog: 3

ARREST JESSE WATSON

by Sgt. Norman Buckner, Indianapolis, Indiana

This is a cop-and-robber story. I was the cop. The robber was named Jesse Watson. We got the order to arrest him. He was wanted in two states for stealing.

I had nabbed Watson once before — two years before this. He was a big guy. He was tough. Most of the time he was in a bad mood. The last report on him said that he was taking drugs.

We got a tip. Jesse Watson might be hiding out at his father's place.

That's right here in town, I thought. I went to check it out with my partner, Don.

When we got to the building, we met Ron Bealey, another cop. The three of us planned what we would do.

Don and Ron went to the front door. I went around to the back. It was raining hard. Over the noise of the rain, I heard them knock. Someone answered. It was Watson. He tried to close the door on them. Then he ran inside.

The place was dark. I had the only flashlight, so Don and Ron called to me. I led the way into the dark room.

I could not find a light switch. So I went on slowly, room by room. The flashlight did not help much. I drew my gun. Watson might be hiding in any corner. Without a sound, I moved ahead. I heard only the rain pounding on the roof. I shivered.

When I got to the back bedroom, I stopped by the door. The light showed a figure on the other side of the bed. He was holding a blanket in front of him. It was Jesse Watson.

He was big. I knew he would be. But the shadows made him look bigger, like some angry giant. At six-foot-two, 220 pounds, he towered over me. I am only five-foot-ten, 160 pounds. He also had a beard. That made him look even more scary.

I thought he might have a club under the blanket. I moved toward him and said, "OK, Jesse, drop it."

"No. You drop it," he said. He dropped the blanket. It was not a club in his hand. It was a shotgun. And it was pointed right at me. If he squeezed the trigger, I would be blown to bits.

My heart beat like a drum. I felt a pounding in my head. But I kept the flashlight steady. And my gun was still pointed at him. I wondered what to do.

He could shoot me at any time, I thought. In my mind, I saw a picture of my wife and our two kids. I had never been so afraid.

Shoot him, I thought, *before he shoots.* But something stopped me. All of a sudden, I found myself praying. "Please help me do the right thing, God."

Don and Ron were waiting outside the room. They were waiting for me to make a move. They knew that Jesse might shoot if he got scared. They thought it was better to let one person handle him. And it was up to me. But if I was so scared, I wondered how scared Jesse must be.

We stood facing each other for a couple of minutes. I was afraid to say a word. It might upset him. My throat was dry. "Give me strength, Lord," I prayed. "I've never been in a mess like this before. I'm trusting in you."

After a few more minutes, I spoke. Softly, I said, "Jesse, your only chance is to come with us."

"No way," he said. He waved the shotgun at me.

More minutes ticked by. He wouldn't move. I wouldn't move. My arms ached. But my eyes slowly got used to the darkness in the room. I saw something on the bed. It was a Bible.

Looking at the Bible, I had a feeling of hope. I prayed, "If your Word is real, God, I need you now."

Then I looked at Jesse. Pointing to the Bible, I said, "What about that?"

"I'm going to church now," he said softly. Then his voice became louder. "And I feel God forgives all my sins."

I had to choose my words with care. "That could be, Jesse," I said. "But first you have to settle things here."

"God is the only judge!" Jesse shouted. "How can any man on earth judge me?"

Slowly, I put my gun down.

"Jesse," I said, "Do you think God wants you to hurt me?"

I bent over to pick up the Bible. But I kept my eye on Jesse. He did not move. I turned the pages. What verse should I read? I heard myself breathing deeply. The pages stopped at Romans 8:18.

"Jesse, listen to this!" I said. "Our suffering now is nothing compared to the glory he will give us later."

Jesse was silent. He had caught the meaning of the verse.

All of a sudden, he shouted, "I can't take jail!"

"Don't try to limit God," I said. "You could serve God in jail. Look at Paul when he was in jail. Or Daniel in the lions' den. You could help others get to know the Lord."

He nodded. But the shotgun was still pointed at me.

I was running out of ideas. I looked at my watch. An hour had passed. I was very tired. I kept praying.

A gunshot ripped through the room. The windows shook. A yellow flash lit up the room. The blast threw me back against the door.

Then I saw what happened. Jesse's finger must have twitched. That touched off the trigger. But the gun was pointed down at the time. It shot a huge hole in the bed.

For a long minute, Jesse did not move. I held my breath. Then he dropped the shotgun to the floor.

I went over and touched him on the arm. He looked at me. There were tears in his eyes. Then he held out his arms so I could put handcuffs on him.

"The Lord sent a man of faith to rescue me," he said. His voice sounded tired. I was tired, too.

Jesse went on. "I have been reading the Bible," he said. "I know that with God's help I'll make it." He said he was sorry for letting the shotgun go off.

He was a new man. And so was I. As scary as that case was, it opened many doors for me. Many of my police friends asked me what happened. I told them all about God. I never opened up like that before.

Now I try to see each new case as a special one. Each person — like Jesse Watson — is a special person. If I can help just one person, that's enough.

READING SCORES:
Flesch-Kincaid: 1
Gunning-Fog: 3

NOWHERE ELSE TO GO

by Donnie Galloway, Gold Hill, North Carolina

I kept thinking about my cousin. I drove my truck for miles. And I kept thinking about him. The two of us had been close. But then he killed himself.

As I drove, I tried to put the thoughts out of my mind. But those thoughts stuck to my mind like a magnet. I felt heavy inside. It was as if someone had put a weight on my shoulders. It was as if someone had kicked me in the stomach.

He was so young. His whole life was ahead of him. I thought back to the times I had talked with him. But we had never talked about death.

It was only two weeks since he had died. I was not able to go to the viewing. I had to work. I am a trucker. My boss would not let me go.

Now it was two weeks later, and I was on the road again. I had to haul a load of bricks down south. It was a gray day. The clouds and showers did nothing to cheer me up.

It was raining as I pulled out of a truck stop south of Charlotte. There was a bridge a few miles ahead. This bridge went over a lovely river. I had to cross that bridge. Then I would be on my way. I did not know how much that bridge would change my life.

As I drove onto the bridge, I saw a sign. It said, "Right Lane Closed — 1,000 Feet Ahead."

Next to me, a lady was driving a small car. I let her pass me. Then I pulled over into the left lane.

All of a sudden, the car stopped. The whole line of cars had stopped. But I couldn't. With my heavy truck, I would skid right into them. I had five tons of metal and ten tons of bricks. All of that would smash into the cars ahead.

"Oh, no!" I thought. "Dear God, I'm going to kill them!" But there was nowhere else to go. Only down, off the bridge.

I knew I had to do it. If I didn't drive off the bridge, I would kill all those people.

I pulled the steering wheel to the right. My truck missed the cars. It headed for the guard rail. I heard metal crash into metal. Then I was falling . . . .

The truck and the bricks and I fell eighty feet. I was afraid. *This is it!* I thought.

We hit the river hard. The windshield broke. Muddy water rushed in. It swept me back. The truck was sinking fast. My tools and sleeping gear were floating around me. I was confused. I could not see.

I reached forward in the blackness. I could hardly move. My lungs were about to burst. I thought I would die right there.

Then I touched the steering wheel. The open
windshield was in front of me. The truck was starting
to spin around. In a moment the windshield would be
facing the river bottom. I had to get out fast.

I kicked. I pushed. I pulled myself through. But then
I was lost. There was more blackness all around me.
Which way was up? I did not know. I just stretched my
arms and began to swim.

In a few moments I hit the river bottom. That's
when I gave up. I thought it was my time to die. I
could only pray.

"Dear God," I said, "go with me. I don't know if
you want me to live or die. But go with me. And please
help those people on the bridge. Don't let anyone be
hurt, please."

I did not feel afraid any more.

Then I felt my body going up. Up, up, up. Ten feet,
twenty, thirty, thirty-five. I was being pushed up.

My head broke the water surface. I saw a boat with
two men. They were coming my way.

I shouted to them. Then I choked on some water and
went down. But I fought my way back to the top. I was
still alive! I fought to stay afloat. Then those men got
to me. They pulled me into the boat.

Lying on the bottom of the boat, I gasped. It felt
good to breathe again.

"Did I hurt any people up there?" I asked. "Are they
all OK?"

We looked up at the bridge. There were flashing lights. There were police and tow trucks. Crowds of people were looking down at us. There were even medics on the scene. *Some people must be hurt badly,* I thought. I was afraid that it was my fault.

The two men moved the boat under the bridge. They called up to the crowd. "How many are hurt up there?"

"We are all fine," someone shouted back. "The medics are here to help the trucker. How is he?"

They looked at me. "He is out of breath," they said. "But he is in pretty good shape."

Good shape. Well, one of my legs may never be the same. And my back bothers me sometimes. But I am still driving trucks. And I still cross that bridge. I always look for that patch in the guard rail. The place where I went through. It reminds me of a lesson I learned at the bottom of the river. I learned something special about life.

I was facing death. At the bottom of that river, there was no way out. But God was with me. I was not afraid of death.

But I learned something else, too. I wish my cousin had learned this. I don't have to be afraid of life either. If you just ask God to go with you, he will. He will lift you up. He will walk with you the rest of the way.

God has a plan for each one of us. He wants us to live. And he will give us the courage to live. We just have to take it.

READING SCORES:
Flesch-Kincaid: 1
Gunning-Fog: 3

THE FEELING
by J. V. Calvert, Fort Worth, Texas

"What is it, Lord?" A strange feeling kept nagging at me. "Why do I feel like something bad is going to happen?"

I was talking to God as I drove. That's normal for me. I was driving my eighteen-wheeler, hauling 48,000 pounds of steel. It was three in the morning.

The truck was fine. I had checked it before I left. The only thing that bothered me was a spider. That's right. I'm six-foot-two. I'm fifty-two years old. But I can't stand spiders. And one of those creepy things had just crawled in front of me. I took a glove and brushed it away.

But something else bothered me, too. I had this strange feeling. My sixth sense was telling me to stay awake. I needed to be very alert. Something was going to happen. I told the Lord about it.

"Lord God," I prayed. "You are my Father. I know you want the best for your children. Now I ask you to ride with me. Sit close to me. Keep me alert. Help me get rid of this crazy feeling. I will give you all the glory."

A lot of truckers talk on their CB radios. That's how they spend their time. I would rather talk to the Lord. I learned that from my parents. Talking to God was as common as breathing. We all would sing with each other. I still do that. Driving late at night, I sing the old hymns. And I pray.

But this night was strange. I just could not relax.

I reached my goal. I dropped off the steel. Then I headed back home with a new load. Now I had 43,000 pounds of bleach. I had to haul this back to a place in Fort Worth.

At 6:45 A.M. I was planning to stop for breakfast. I always ate at the Dixie Cafe. So I pulled in there and parked. But that feeling still troubled me. "Don't stop now," a voice seemed to say. "Keep moving down the road."

I sat still for a few seconds. I tried to resist. I was thinking about juice and eggs and coffee. But the feeling was too strong. I started up the truck and got back on the road.

"Something strange is going on in your head," I told myself. "I can handle this truck just fine. But this feeling is strange!"

Then I turned it over to the Lord. "Please, Lord, I'm counting on you. Stay with me."

Out on Highway 6, I kept my eyes on the road. It was only two lanes wide. I had to be careful. Still, I began to sing. "Jesus loves me, this I know. For the Bible tells me so." I hadn't sung that since I was a kid.

About thirty miles later, I saw a truck behind me. He was moving fast. He must have had an empty truck. Since I had a heavy load, I was going slow. I pulled over to let him pass me. The truck zoomed by. The driver raised his hand to thank me. Soon he was 300 yards ahead.

And then it happened. That big rig went out of control. It reeled along the wrong side of Highway 6. It bounced along the shoulder of the road. Then it flipped over. I heard something explode. Then fire and smoke were coming from the cab.

My truck was parked a safe distance away. But I ran toward the crash. I pumped my legs as fast as they could go. "O Lord, have mercy," I prayed. I rushed toward the fire.

When I saw the driver, I thought he was dead. His head was bleeding. He had been thrown through the side window. His shoulders were stuck in the metal braces of his side mirror.

"O Lord, have mercy!" I prayed again. "Give me power to yank those braces loose."

Then the man moaned. He was alive! I took a deep breath. Then I grabbed the braces of that mirror. I pulled as hard as I could. It came loose! But I still had to get him out of the truck.

"Please, God," I prayed in my head. "Help us! Don't let him be stuck in this fire."

"You have to try to help me, Buddy," I told the man. His arms were pinned to his sides. But he began to move.

"That's it! Keep wiggling!" I pulled his body through the side window.

"Please, God," I prayed again. "Help us get away before the gas tanks explode!"

I helped the man to his feet. He began to walk. But he was in shock. He was covered with blood, dirt, and broken glass. He fell down after a few steps. We were still too close.

Then I looked up. Something strange was going on. The wind was blowing from the south. It should have been blowing the fire right at us. But it wasn't. Instead, the smoke went straight up. Then it went over us. It came down in the middle of the road. It was like a rainbow. It was going right over us!

I helped the man to his feet again. We rushed about fifty yards away. Then the gas tanks blew. The whole truck went up in flames.

"Thank you, Almighty Lord!" I prayed.

People came from all over. Some tried to fight the fire. Others gathered around us. Soon the medics were there. They started to take care of the driver. My job was done.

I walked back to my truck. But someone caught up with me. "Hey, you saved that man's life," he said. "No one else had the guts to go near that truck. It could have blown at any second."

I shook my head. "I don't want any credit," I said. "I just try to stay close to the Lord. When I need help, he's there to give it. And he pushed me to help this other man today."

I thought for a minute and began to laugh. "You think I've got guts? You are looking at a man who's scared of a little spider!"

READING SCORES:
Flesch-Kincaid: 1
Gunning-Fog: 3

GOD, LET ME RAISE MY KIDS!
by Betty Cusack, Bronx, New York

I was tired, but happy. I had five children to take care
of. Since I lost my husband, I had to do it alone. But
God helped me find a job. And he was helping me
raise my kids. God was good.

One winter morning, I was driving home. I got off
the highway and took a side street. That street was on a
hill. And on this cold morning, it was covered with ice.
I stopped at the top of the hill. From there I looked
down the icy street.

Just then a car came up behind me. It banged into
my car. That sent me sliding down the hill. The other
car slid down behind me.

It was like a game of bumper cars — only very scary.
My car bounced from one side of the street to the other.
I hit parked cars on the sides. I spun around and around.
Other cars came over the hill and slid down, too. These
cars hit mine on the way down. First one hit me. Then
another car hit me. In all, five cars smashed into mine.

At last, my car stopped at the bottom of the hill. It
was all smashed in.

I heard glass crash. I tasted blood. But I thought of my kids. "Dear God," I prayed. "All I want to do is raise my children. Then I'll be ready to die, if you want."

Then I went blank. When I came to, I was the only one around. Someone walked by and saw me. He said the police had come. They had taken away all the others who were hurt. But they thought I was dead. They only had room for the living.

I'm alive! I thought. *I'm alive!* I snapped my fingers to prove it. O Lord, thank you for hearing my prayer!

God made me strong enough to get up. He helped me walk home through the snow. I didn't even know I was hurt. I just kept saying to myself, "I have to get home. I have to fix supper for the kids." I was in shock. I know that now. I should have waited for the police to come back.

But I thought I was fine. The next day I was talking on the phone with my sister. I was telling her about the crash. All of a sudden I felt strange.

"Come get me!" I yelled. "I'm going numb!"

She got there soon. I could not move the left side of my body. A few minutes later, I could not talk.

Soon doctors and nurses were standing over me. They said my neck was broken. They said my back was hurt vert badly. They said my insides were cut and bleeding.

"Dear Lord," I wanted to shout. "I feel too good to be dying. Tell them for me, please." I still could not talk.

I lay there for two days. Nothing changed. People buzzed around me. I heard them say I might not make it. I heard them say I would never talk or walk again. I began to see how badly I was hurt .

Lying there, I started to feel sorry for myself. But as I thought about it, I felt better. My life had brought some bad things. My husband's death was hard to take. Raising five kids was not easy. But God did not make me a quitter! When I lost my husband, I went right to God.

"Lord, I don't have a penny," I said. "I guess you'll have to show me what to do. Tell me how to raise these kids the way you want." And God did.

I was praying again now. I still could not talk out loud. God was the only one who could hear me. But he always does.

"If I have to live like this," I told God, "take me away now. But I know you want me to raise my kids. I'm not quitting on you yet, Lord."

I opened my eyes and saw a doctor. He was pointing at me. "This one's amazing," he said. "Walked for miles with a broken neck."

Yes! I thought. When God helped me then, he was sending a message. "Betty," he was saying, "you can pull through this, too."

The next day people were around me again. "What a shame!" they said. "She'll never get better." I guess they didn't know how great my God was. I felt I had to say something. I had to show them that God was helping me. I just had to!

My face got red. My jaw got tight. My mouth opened. And words came out!

"I'm — going — back — to — work," I said. Now they were the ones who couldn't talk. They didn't know what to say. But it was true. I had to go back to work. I had to take care of my kids.

I thought back to the time right after my husband died. I knew I had to work. But it was hard to find a good job. And it was hard to find baby-sitters. Then one day, when I felt like giving up, I prayed. I asked God to find an answer for me. Just then a lady rang the doorbell. She was from Stanley Home Products. Stanley needed workers. She was trying to find people who would sell their products.

"Maybe you can help me . . . ," she began to say.

"Maybe you can help me!" I said. I asked her in. *My,* I thought, *the Lord works fast.* This job was perfect. I could work on my own time. I could even take my kids along. I started selling right away. By the time of the crash, I was leading the area in sales.

But now I was in trouble. "Lord, I'm always in trouble," I prayed. "How am I going to earn a living from this bed?"

It was almost as if the Lord's voice came to me. "I gave you one job. How many do you want?" So I started selling Stanley Products from my bed. God had given me my voice back. Now I could sell again.

My bosses from Stanley brought me some products. I showed these to the doctors and nurses. I taught them how to use the creams and soaps. And I made a lot of sales. I even moved to a larger ward, so I could sell to other patients. Soon I was making almost as much money as before.

"Lord," I said, "thank you. But I don't just want to make money for my kids. I want to raise them. I need to go home. I need to walk."

The doctors were saying I would never walk. They just made me mad. "How can you say that?" I would say. "Are you my Master? I have a God who says I can walk."

This was about a month after the crash. A nurse came by. She was taking me to the X-ray room. She brought a wheel-chair.

"Take this thing away," I said. "I'm going to walk."

The nurse's mouth fell open. "Now Betty . . . ," she said.

But I just closed my eyes and prayed. "Please, God. Let me walk now."

I pushed myself to my feet. I felt dizzy. I swayed. But I held onto the wall. The nurse stood by to help.

"Betty, won't you sit . . . ," she said.

I shook my head. "Please, God. You didn't make me a quitter." I took my hands off the wall. Other people were watching me now. There wasn't a sound. I put out my right foot. I held my breath. Then I dragged my left foot forward. It hurt very badly. But I stood there on both feet.

Then I fell down.

"Thank you, Lord," I prayed. "I knew you could do it." I had taken my first step.

I took more steps in the next few days. My legs were moving slowly. But they were moving! The doctors gave me a neck brace. And just three months after the crash, I was home.

I hugged my kids. I kissed them. We cried with joy. Then I saw a pile of boxes on the floor. Stanley Home Products. "Lord," I said, "you don't let up. Do you?"

And I started selling right away. I went to people's homes. My kids helped me carry the boxes. I laughed and kidded with people. And they helped me.

I wore that neck brace for four years. Sometimes it was hard to roll out of bed. But I said to myself, "Betty, shape up! The Lord has done so much for you. The least you can do is get out of bed."

The pain never went away. But I would not give in to it. I was the best mother I could be. And I kept selling.

Three years ago, I got married to a very nice man. I also got a better job at Stanley. Now I'm in charge of twenty-eight people.

Sometimes these people come to me with problems. They are sad or troubled. They feel they can't go on. I tell them, "Look here! The only way you can lose is to quit on life. Life never quits on you. But just living is not enough. You have to spend time with God, too.

"Without him, I'd still be in bed. I would have no voice. I would not be able to walk. I would be lying there feeling sorry for myself. With his help, I have my legs. And I have my voice. Now I can walk and work and sing. Now I can thank God for his blessings.

"I am alive! And I'm not quitting!"

READING SCORES:
Flesch-Kincaid: 1
Gunning-Fog: 3

HIDDEN DANGER

by S. Richard Pastorella, New York, New York

"Thank you, Lord. You give me strength to live each
new day."

That was the prayer I said to God each new day. I prayed
it until I reached the age of forty-two. Then I stopped. I felt
that God had been unfair to me. I thought my life was over.

As a child, I was true to God. My parents taught me
to love God and trust him. One sight of my father still
sticks with me. He was a tough, blue-collar worker.
But once I saw him looking at a lovely sunset. He
slowly knelt down to worship the God who made it.
That was the kind of people we were. Loving. Trusting.

And that was the kind of home I wanted. I married a
woman named Mary. We had two sons. By then I was
on the New York police force. I did well. I won
awards. They gave me better and better jobs. Then I
made a major choice. I joined the bomb squad.

"Why?" Mary asked me. Again and again she asked,
"Why?"

I tried to explain. "Any cop faces danger at any
time. There are times when I've almost been killed.

And the bomb squad has its dangers, too. But I know the danger. I know what and when it is. I can trust my skill to keep me safe." We both knew that I also trusted God.

For eighteen months, things went fine. We went out on about seventy-five calls. Most of these came after a bomb went off. But then came New Year's Eve, 1982.

I was eating a snack with my partner, Tony. It was a slow night. So far. Then we got a call. A bomb had gone off. We rushed downtown to check it out. We picked up the pieces. We were happy that no one was hurt. But then we got a new report. A bomb had gone off three blocks away. At a police station. We rushed over there.

A man was lying on the floor. He was bloody, but still awake. I bent over him.

"What did the bomb look like?" I asked. I knew there might be other bombs around.

"In . . . in a . . . in a bag." The man was in pain. "A bag . . . like . . . Chicken Delight." He started to get up. I put my coat over him. I didn't want him to see that one of his legs was gone.

The medics came to take the man away. Tony and I said a short prayer for him. Then we moved through the building. We had to see if there were other bombs.

We had a dog to help us. He was named High Hat. He was trained to sniff for bombs. If he found one, he would sit down.

The dog pulled Tony toward two pillars. Two paper bags lay there. High Hat sat down.

Two bombs had gone off. There might be two more here. We needed more men. Tony went to phone for backup. A radio signal could set off a live bomb.

People began to gather around. I asked the other police to move them away. They moved High Hat, too. Tony came back and got behind me. I said a short prayer as I reached for the first bag.

That is all I know.

I woke up in a bed. Doctors were around me. My head was wrapped. My ears roared. The pain was awful.

Even with all that pain, I thought it would pass. I would be OK. God would make sure of that.

But a week later I learned the truth. Tony had lost an eye. He also lost some hearing. My face and right arm were badly burned. My right hand had no fingers, only stumps. My right ear could not hear. My left ear could hear only a little. One eye was gone. I was blind in the other. My career was over. Now I was no good at all. No one would want me. Why had God done this to me?

I got a phone call from Ronald Reagan. Even that didn't cheer me up.

"Nancy and I are praying for you," he said. "This is a great loss for you. But I know God has something good in store. Hang on to that thought. If it isn't clear now, it will be soon."

I thanked him for his words. But they couldn't give me back my sight. How was I going to get my life in order?

At last I got home. I tried to do each thing as I had before. This just made me feel worse. I had been right-handed. Now I had to use my left hand to button my shirt. This was hard. Sometimes I got so upset, I ripped the shirt. I could do very little by myself. I could not even read my mail. I tried to go to church, just like before. But it was just a habit. Inside, I was very mad at God.

At first, other police came to see me. But soon they stopped. I don't blame them. When they saw me, they thought about themselves. The same thing might happen to them.

In time I learned to dress myself. I learned to write, to walk, even to cook.

But one night I was talking with Mary. Tony and his wife, Carole, were with us. I felt a lot of pity for myself. I let it all out. "Is this all that's left? Learning to dress myself? Learning to fry an egg? Waiting for a phone call? Trying to think about the way it was before? Is this what God wants for me? For the rest of my life?"

Then Mary said something I had never heard before. "You're not the only one who is hurt," she said. "Carole and I hurt, too. Not like you and Tony, but we hurt."

"And there are other cops who have been hurt," Carole added. "You're not the only ones."

Those words turned around in my head all night. Mary and Carole were right. I was thinking only of myself. I forgot about those around me. And what about all the other cops who were hurt?

The next day I wrote to some police chiefs. I asked for a list of cops hurt in the line of duty. An idea was growing in my head. Maybe if we talked with each other, it would help. We would show each other that we weren't just junk. We could help each other feel better.

I got the list — and a place where we could meet.

And then we met. We found it easy to talk with each other. We knew what the others were feeling. We had been there, too. And we knew we all needed God's help.

We called ourselves The Police Self-Support Groups. Some of us went to see other cops who had just been hurt. We got the police to pay our doctors' bills on time. We helped wives to get to know what their husbands were feeling. We helped children to deal with their fears.

One of our men was Don Rios. He had been shot in the back. He was in a wheelchair. He was told he could never father a child. He was coming apart. So was his marriage. We got a doctor to help get their marriage straight. Now they are going to have their first child. Don is walking now. And he visits other cops in need.

It's an old cure for self-pity, I guess. Get out of yourself. Do something for someone else. But it worked. As I went to church, I found that I wanted to be there. It was not just habit. I wanted to worship God.

No, the Lord did not leave me when the bomb went off. That's what I thought at first. But he was saying, "I have other work for you, Don. But you will have to go through some pain. Then you can help others who are hurting."

God is leading me to help others. In that way, he is helping me. He gave me back my faith. In that way, he has healed me. I really believe that.

"Thank you, Lord. You give me strength to live each new day." I am saying that prayer again. Each new day.

READING SCORES:
Flesch-Kincaid: 1
Gunning-Fog: 4

KIDNAP!

by Eunice Peterson Kronholm, Lino Lakes, Minnesota

It was about eight o'clock on a cold Friday morning. I stepped outside. The March air seemed bright and clear. I had been down with the flu all week, so I was bundled up. But even with my coat and scarf, I shivered.

My husband, Gunnar, had left for work at the bank. Now I was headed out to get my hair done. I began to scrape ice from my car windshield.

There were noises behind me. I turned and saw two men in ski masks. One pointed a gun at me. I screamed, but it did no good.

We live in the suburbs. But our house is set apart from the other houses. No neighbors were around to hear.

The two men grabbed me and forced me into my car. "Do what we say and you won't get hurt," said one. I was stiff with fear. The men put a blindfold on me. They tied my hands. Then they threw me into the back seat.

I felt the car backing out of the driveway. "What do you want?" I asked.

"We'll tell you later!"

I thought about how helpless I was. There was no one at home to help. Our children are grown. They have all moved away. Gunnar didn't expect to hear from me until two o'clock. I found myself praying, "Father, I trust you to watch over me."

In the back seat of the car, I twisted and turned. Then the men stopped and moved me to a new car. After driving some more, we entered a garage. They led me up some stairs and into a room. I peeked under my blindfold. The room had a white shag rug.

"Sit down here," a voice said.

"Please," I said. "What do you want?"

"Money — from your husband."

Of course. Gunnar was president of a bank in South St. Paul.

"Where can we reach him?" asked one of the men.

I gave him the number. "If everyone plays along," he said, "this should only take a few hours."

One man left the room. The other sat next to me. I could sense how tense he was. I thought about others who had been kidnapped — and killed. I began to worry. But then a Bible verse came to my mind.

"Don't be afraid, for I am with you." That's what God said to Isaiah. "Don't be afraid, for I am with you. . . . I will strengthen you" (Isaiah 41:10). The Bible also says God "will keep in perfect peace all those who trust in him" (Isaiah 26:3).

My fear slipped away. My senses got clearer. I work as a nurse, and I teach a class in mental health. So I thought the best thing was to keep calm. I would talk calmly to the man.

I tried to sound happy. "Well, I don't want to talk to the wall," I said. "So I'll call you Bill, OK?"

At first he kept quiet. Then he said softly, "OK."

"How much will you ask for?"

"Half a million," he said.

Half a million dollars! My heart sank.

"I don't know if my husband can get that," I said.

"He'd better!" snapped Bill. His voice was ugly.

I prayed for Gunnar, my husband. Then I rubbed my wrists, where they had been tied.

Bill leaned over to me. My nose picked up his rough smell. "You're a cool one," he said. "How come you're so calm?"

"Because I believe God is protecting me," I answered.

He was silent. But it seemed that he cared what I had to say. So I told him how Christ had changed my life. Jesus gave me a whole new set of values, I said. The man kept quiet. Still, I thought I sensed a change in him.

It was now about noon, I figured. Bill gave me some coffee. I still had the blindfold on, but I could hear the radio. It was picking up police calls.

Later that day, the other man guarded me. I tried to talk to him, too.

"I called the other man Bill," I said. "What can I call you?"

"Jerry will do," he said.

We sat there for hours. My body was very sore. *By now they must have talked to Gunnar,* I thought. *Surely they will let me go soon.*

I forced myself to talk to Jerry. I asked him about his family. Then he turned to me, just as Bill had done. "How come you're so relaxed?"

"God gives me strength," I said. I tried to keep my voice from shaking. "I believe that he is keeping me safe. Do you want me to tell you about it?"

He jumped to his feet and walked away. "No!" he snapped.

The minutes ticked slowly away. It was now evening. Bill came back.

"Have you talked to my husband?" I asked. Bill just mumbled something about being double-crossed. "You'll have to spend the night here," he said.

Here? Tears came to my eyes. But God brought his words to my mind again. "God is our refuge and strength. He is a tested help in times of trouble" (Psalm 46:1).

Now I felt pains from hunger. I had not eaten since breakfast. Jerry gave me a tiny bit of a sandwich. He said it was all he had.

I slept that night on the rug. The next morning every bone in my body ached. Both men seemed to be in a bad mood. Their plan was not working.

And still there was nothing to eat or drink. At noon they gave me a can of soda pop.

Then, late on Saturday, Bill said, "We'll have to move you." They took me to the garage. The icy air bit into me. I heard the car trunk open.

"Please!" I cried. "Not the trunk!"

"It's the only way," Bill said. The two men pushed me in and slammed the lid. I curled around the spare tire as the car bumped along. Hours passed. I cried in pain from cramps and the cold. Then we stopped. Still in my blindfold, I was led into a small room.

They gave me a stale hot dog bun. I ate half of it and saved the rest. Two days had passed. Would I ever see my husband again? But God brought his words to me again. "He [God] will never let me stumble, slip, or fall. For he is always watching, never sleeping" (Psalm 121:3-4).

Sunday morning Jerry guarded me. Bill left. I was coughing from the flu. Jerry turned on the radio.

"Can you get KTIS?" I asked.

KTIS is a Christian station. Soon I heard a hymn being sung in a church service. It was First Baptist Church. I knew the pastor there and his wife. It made me feel at home, at least a little bit. Then a speaker said, "We are asking people to pray for Eunice Kronholm. Ask God to bring her home safely." They were praying for me! That made me feel much better.

For Sunday dinner, I had a can of soda pop. Later that day, Bill and Jerry let me take off my blindfold.

For a short time, at least. They made me write to my husband. The note told him how to pay the ransom money.

That night they tied me up. Then both of them left to pick up the money. I lay there sick with fear. All of a sudden Bill came back and said, "We've got to move." He put me in the car again.

Maybe I'm going home! That's what I thought. But after driving a while, we parked. I was led into the room with the shag rug. The whole mess was starting all over again!

Jerry came back and Bill left. "When am I going to go home?" I asked.

"I don't know." Jerry seemed quiet, as if things were not going well.

I had a new thought. I had been praying for God to keep me safe. And he had! Now maybe I should ask God to let me go by a certain time. The hour of six o'clock came to my mind. "Oh, God," I prayed, "take me home by six o'clock tonight."

That helped me relax. "Jerry," I said, "I don't know what you think is going to happen. But I feel that God is going to get me home by six o'clock."

He didn't answer. On the radio, the music stopped. A news report came on. "A suspect in the Kronholm case has just been caught."

Jerry was upset. Once again, I was afraid. *Is this how it will happen?* I thought. *Will he shoot me now?*

But a new Bible verse stopped me. I had been dwelling on the bad things that might happen. But Paul wrote that we should think about the good things. "Fix your thoughts on what is true and good and right. Think about things that are pure and lovely. Dwell on the fine, good things in others" (Philippians 4:8).

Now I tried to talk Jerry into letting me go. "I'll get some money for you," I said.

"No," he said. "It won't work." He kept pacing the floor. The radio said it was after five.

"Why don't you let me go now?" I asked.

Jerry just looked out the window. "Well," he said, "wait until dark."

Until dark? I was too weak to walk in the dark. I talked to Jerry some more. Then I said, "I think I'll put my coat on."

"OK," Jerry sighed. "You might as well take off your blindfold, too." Something was falling apart inside of him.

I stood up to leave. When I took off the blindfold, the light hurt my eyes. When I got used to it, I could see the room around me. And I saw Jerry. He looked very sad.

"You know," he said, "I have never met a woman like you. You don't seem to feel bitter toward us."

I looked into his sad eyes. "I'm not bitter," I said, "really. I forgive you. God loves you."

I turned and stepped outside. The sun was going down. I began to walk down the road. There were trees all around. I heard Jerry behind me. But I kept walking. I got to a highway and looked back. I couldn't see Jerry at all.

"Oh, Father," I prayed, "send a car, please." Soon a car came by. I waved my arms to flag it down. The driver took me to a store. From there, I called home. My fingers shook as I dialed the phone. One of our sons answered. Our three children had come to our home. They were praying for me there.

Soon, the FBI men came and took me to Gunnar. We fell into each other's arms. A few minutes later I looked at my watch. It was 6:10 P.M.

READING SCORES:
Flesch-Kincaid: 1
Gunning-Fog: 4

OUT OF THE SKY
by Steve Davis, Dallas, Texas

No one could fly a plane in this weather. Clouds were hanging low in the sky. I sat with my friends at the airport in Portland, Texas. It was a small airport in a small town. We would not see any planes that day. We were sure of that.

But we were wrong. A plane dropped out of the sky that day. It landed at our airport. And it changed my life. But let me go back to the start of the story.

A year before this, I had moved to Texas. I came from the east. I didn't have much money when I came. But I got a job teaching people to fly. Now I had my own flight school. I even had three airplanes of my own.

One of the first people I taught was Linda. She was a lovely young woman. Soon she became my girlfriend.

I had it made. I had more money than I needed. I had friends at the airport. I had a girlfriend. But there was still a nagging feeling inside of me. I felt empty.

On this gray day, I sat with my friends at the airport. I went out to the Chicken Shack to get some lunch.

Then the other guys and I just talked. It was hard enough driving through this rain and fog. Surely no one would be flying.

We ate and we talked. There were four of us. Jess, Ray, A.A., and myself. A.A. was sixty years old. He was just learning to fly. Jess and Ray kidded him for starting so late in life.

"Better late than never," A.A. said. "But I'm not like Steve. I bet he could fly before he could walk."

He was talking about me. My dad worked as a pilot for a Christian mission. I spent most of my early years in Mexico. Talking with my friends, I thought about those early years. When I was ten, it was great to ride with my dad. We would ride to the airport on those dusty roads. Then we would climb into our airplane. It was a hunk of junk, really. But my dad put a new engine in it. It had lots of power. And it made lots of noise.

"Let's load her up, Steve," my dad would call. We would load the plane with boxes of supplies. Then we would strap ourselves in. Each time we took off, it was a thrill. It was also very scary. But then we would be in the open skies. We would fly over mountains and forests.

Dad would even pretend to fall asleep. Then I would have to keep the plane on course. He would take the controls again and land the plane. We were always dropping into some small village. The people in these

places were always happy to see us. They were eager
to get the supplies we brought.

Jess, Ray, and A.A. started talking about something
else. But my mind stayed in that village.

Dad and I would unload the supplies. Then he would
gather the people around him. Dad told them about
Jesus. I liked to listen to him. Jesus Christ was very
real to me back then. I wanted to grow up and be a
mission pilot, too.

Once my parents gave me a book. It was called
Through Gates of Splendor. It was the story of five men
on a mission to a mountain village in Ecuador. They
were killed by the people in the village. It was a moving
story of faith. But the best part, I thought, was about
the pilot. His name was Nate Saint. He was my hero.

Sometimes, as I flew with my dad, I thought of Nate
Saint. I would pretend that I was Nate Saint.

Things had changed since then. As I thought about
those days, I felt empty again. As a boy, I had a lot of
faith. I trusted God. I was ready to give my life to God,
just like Nate Saint. But somewhere along the line . . .
something had happened.

I was an adult now. I had adult things to worry
about. I had doubts. I was tempted. There were no
other Christians around to help me with these doubts.
So I just let them be. I stopped thinking about my faith.
I only thought about flying. Where my faith had once
been, there was now a sense of loss. I was empty.

A few months before, I had come across that book. *Through Gates of Splendor* caught my eye. I tried to put it away, but I couldn't. Sadness gripped me. I thought back to the faith I once had. Then I said the first prayer I had said in years.

"Now wait a minute, God," I said. "Something tells me you are not real. I wish I could know you now like I did then. I wish I could have my old faith back. But I can't accept all those things now. If you let me know you are real, I will serve you. But I have to know for sure. I can't pretend."

I thought that God might answer me right away. He didn't. I didn't feel any new faith. That made me angry.

"So it is all a joke," I thought. "My old hero, Nate Saint, died in vain."

The book had fallen open. There were pictures in the center. I was looking at a picture of Nate's son, Steve. At the time of the picture, he was five years old. "He would be about my age now," I thought. "And I bet he is in even worse shape than I am. He probably has even worse doubts than I do."

I put the book away. I was angry. That was a few months before this gray day at the airport. But I was still angry.

The guys were still talking. I tried to forget about my doubts. What would the guys think? If they knew I was looking for answers from God, they would laugh.

"Well, the rain's getting worse," Jess said. "We should close up."

All of a sudden, one of the workers came in. "Look!" he said in Spanish. "A plane is coming!"

We looked out through the rain. Sure enough, a small plane had dropped through the clouds. It was going to land here.

For a moment we were worried, but the plane landed safely. "I bet they are drug runners," said Ray. "Who else would fly on a day like today?"

Two young men got out of the plane. They both looked clean-cut. The two came into the office.

"Hello," said the pilot. "We barely made it. I didn't think I would find a place to land. Can we tie down here? Is there a motel in town where we can stay?"

"We were just closing," said Jess. "But you can tie down." A.A. and Ray were on their way out.

"There's a motel in town," I said. "If you hurry, I can drive you over there."

Julio came back in. He's the worker who saw the plane come in. He liked to talk with me. I was the only one around who knew Spanish.

"The weather is bad," said Julio, in Spanish.

The pilot stopped on his way out. In Spanish, he said, "Yes, it's awful out there. I should not have been flying."

The three of us talked for a few minutes. It seemed strange. This blonde-haired, blue-eyed pilot was speaking Spanish very well.

"Where did you learn to speak Spanish?" I asked.

"My parents were mission workers in Ecuador," he said. "I grew up there."

"Really," I said. "Did you ever hear of those men who were killed?"

The pilot's friend spoke up. "One of them was his dad."

"Oh, yeah?" I said. "What's your name?"

"Steve Saint," the pilot said.

He was the boy from the book!

I felt like someone had punched me in the chest. The book had started my faith when I was a boy. But now I had doubts. Now this boy flew out of the book to see me!

But I still wondered. Did he have any faith in God? Or was this just a bad joke?

It was a few minutes before I could talk. I tried to be cool. "You guys could save your motel bill. I live a mile from here. You could stay at my place."

"That would be great," said Steve.

I talked for hours with Steve and his friend. I asked him about his faith. Did he still believe in God?

He told me that he did. His father's death just made his faith stronger. But I kept asking questions. I did not say a word about the book. I did not say that his father had been my hero. I fired my hardest questions at him. "How can you believe this . . . ? What makes you say that . . . ?" My anger came out. But he answered each question with calm faith.

It was a relief to ask these questions. I was letting out my doubts. And Steve Saint showed me that God was real. God is real enough to handle my doubts!

The next day the weather cleared. Steve and his friend took off. I stood alone on the runway. I was a new man. God had answered my prayer. He had given me a new joy.

That was over ten years ago. Now Linda and I are married. Jesus is very real to both of us. Sometimes we fly as mission pilots. We carry supplies to needy villages. And we share our faith with the people there. It's a faith that Nate Saint gave his life for. And, because of one small airplane, that faith is mine, too.

READING SCORES:
Flesch-Kincaid: 1
Gunning-Fog: 4

LIFELINES
by Cathy Baldridge, Millstadt, Illinois

It was a strange few days.

First, there was the weather on Friday. I looked out the kitchen window at dark clouds. The voice on the radio said there might be a twister. To be safe, I took the kids down to the basement. There were four of them. I have two children of my own. Dawn is three. Jeremy is just one. And I was baby-sitting for two other kids.

They all seemed scared as we huddled in the basement. So I told them a story.

My parents were in a German prison camp in World War II. It was an awful place. It was cold. There was little to eat. And in the last few months of the war, it was very scary. Bombs were falling all around.

Most of those in the camp were afraid. At first, my mom and dad were frightened, too. There was no safe place to hide.

But my parents did not give in to the fear. Instead, they prayed and sang hymns. Others shouted, "What are you doing? Are you crazy?" But my parents knew that God was their only hope.

That was the story I told. Then we heard the rain falling outside. We knew we would be OK. No twister today.

"You see," I said. "We don't have to be afraid of the weather. We can ask God to keep us safe. He will answer us."

We said a prayer. Then the kids went upstairs. They went back to their playing. I went back to fixing dinner.

I thought about my parents. That story always makes me think. God was very near to my parents. Why wasn't he near to me? My father was so full of faith. So was my mother. Why wasn't I?

But think of all they went through! Many bad things had happened to them. These things made their faith stronger. I haven't gone through those things.

Then I thought of the things I had gone through. Dawn got very sick when she was a baby. She nearly died. Jeremy had ear problems. My husband, Ray, lost his hearing in one ear. For ten months, he did not have a job.

But these things seemed so common. They were boring problems. God had not been very real in these times. At least not to me.

Ray came home for dinner. I tried to keep the kids quiet so Ray could relax. After dinner, I taught a music lesson. But my student was bored. So was I. I was still thinking about my parents. And my dull life.

The weekend came and went. I had things I planned to do. I just didn't get around to them. In church, my mind wandered.

Monday brought a whole new set of chores. But I didn't feel like doing them. I knew I should stop and read the Bible. God's words could help me out of this slump. But the day went on. I didn't stop.

When Ray come home, he looked bad. Something had happened. He was shaken up.

"On my way home, I saw a crash happen," he said. "It was right in front of me. A car crashed into the guard rail. There was a couple in the car, and a young child. I stopped when I saw it. I tried to settle them down until help came. The father was hurt, but I think he'll be OK. Still, it was pretty scary."

"It was good that you stopped," I said.

"It was the least I could do," he answered.

"But still," I said again, "it was good."

I wanted to stay with Ray. But I had to go shopping. I was supposed to pick up my mom at work.

The kids went with me. As we walked out the door, Ray called to us. "Please be careful, Cathy. Extra careful."

I dropped Dawn off for baton lessons. Then Jeremy and I went to pick up my mother. Jeremy was strapped into his car seat. He soon fell asleep. I drove along. Traffic was not very heavy.

As we got to a railroad crossing, red lights began to flash. The gates came down. We stopped. "Oh, dear," I said. "If it's a long train, we may be late."

I heard a horn honking behind me. In my mirror, I saw a car coming fast. The woman at the wheel honked again. "Where do you want me to go, lady?" I said.

It looked as if she was going to pass me. She was going to try to sneak around the gate and across the tracks. "Fine," I thought. I looked down at Jeremy. He was still sleeping.

All of a sudden, I felt a jolt. The other car crashed into mine. We went spinning, sliding against the crossing gate.

Jeremy was screaming. I reached down to pick him up. But the woman's car hit us again. She pushed us right onto the tracks.

Poor Jeremy was still screaming. I was sure he had broken his neck. I felt his neck and back with my hands. Thank God! He was all in one piece.

The next thing I heard made me freeze. I was scared stiff. It was a train whistle. The train was still out of sight. But it was not far off. It was just around the bend.

I tried to open my door. But it was smashed. And the other car was pinned against it. It would not open. I yelled to the other driver, "Back up!"

She tried to start her car. But the front end was smashed in. It would not start. The woman got out of her car and walked away.

I was crazy with fear. I looked for a way out. The door on the other side! I reached across Jeremy to try it. No. It was pinned against the gatepost.

The train whistle blew again. "Why won't someone help us?" I screamed.

I tried to huddle with Jeremy in the back seat. I would try to protect my baby. I knew it might be useless. But that was all I could think of.

A voice came from outside. "Get out! Get out! You have to get out!"

"We can't," I screamed. "We're trapped."

A brown-haired woman came to the window. She was about my age, and very small. "Get out!" she said again. "Look, you've got to!"

Then I saw it. Its headlight was shining. Its whistle was blowing. The huge, dark train came around the bend. It was only a few hundred yards away. I wanted to hear its brakes screeching. But I didn't.

The woman grabbed the car door. It was still jammed shut. She pulled at it with all she had. It opened five or six inches.

"That's the best I can do," she said. "You'll have to squeeze through."

I tried to unstrap Jeremy from his car seat. My fingers felt like dead sticks. "Please, Lord," I prayed. "Don't let me lose my mind now!"

I got Jeremy loose. Then I crawled over to the door. I tried to squeeze through the narrow slot. It wouldn't work. We didn't fit.

I called to the woman. "Please take my baby!"

"All right," she said. "Give him to me."

I pressed Jeremy through the gap. The woman grabbed him. She took him to safety. I heard his cries trail away. *At least he will live,* I thought.

The train was about fifty feet away. I was all alone. It looked like a monster, huge and scary. It roared. *Why isn't it stopping?* I was twisting in my car, trying to get out. A man was trying to flag the train down. I saw the woman holding my baby. She was still calling to me. "Lord, let me live," I prayed. "For Jeremy's sake. For Dawn. For Ray."

I closed my eyes and twisted again. One more time I would try to squeeze through.

All of a sudden, I was free. It stunned me. But I heard the roaring train behind me. I had to run. I cleared the tracks and looked back. The train was smashing my car.

The sight put me in a daze. People took me across the street to a Dairy Queen. They sat me down. They put Jeremy back in my arms. I thought about the woman who helped me. I hadn't thanked her. Where was she? No one knew. The next day I learned her name: Joyce Johnson.

Jeremy and I were fine. The doctors sent us home. As I told Ray the story, it frightened me again. We came so close to death! I told Ray about the woman who helped us.

Ray said, "We should thank God for her. He puts good people like that in bad places."

Thank God. I do thank God for Joyce Johnson. I am safe now because God rescued me. Just as he had rescued my parents. In my case, he used Joyce Johnson to rescue me. He helped her to open that door.

And then I thought about other times. God was always putting good people in bad places. When my kids were sick, there were cheerful nurses. When Ray lost his job, there were helpful friends. And that same day, God had used Ray. Ray had helped the people in that crash.

It is clear. When you are in pain, God sends good people to help. They are God's lifelines. Through them, God is very real to me now.

READING SCORES:
Flesch-Kincaid: 1
Gunning-Fog: 4

THE DOOR
by Robert L. Daugherty, Dansville, New York

I took off my glasses and smiled. My sister and her husband were fixing up their living room for Christmas. The room looked lovely. My wife, Harriet, and I enjoyed the scene.

They had asked us to join them for Christmas. We lived in New York state. My sister and her husband lived in Dallas, Texas. They had a fancy place in a tall building. And they lived on the fourteenth floor.

"We have lots of room," they told us. "Come and join us." We had no other plans. And we didn't want to spend Christmas alone. So we said yes. And there we were, in their living room, trimming the tree. We laughed together and smiled. It was the day before Christmas Eve.

Late that night, Harriet and I were sleeping soundly in the guest room. All of a sudden, we heard a scream. It was my sister's husband.

"Wake up!" he yelled. "There's a fire!"

We got out of bed right away. It was very dark. But when we opened the door, we saw the living room. It looked orange. The place was still dark, but the fire made an orange glow.

"We will look for a fire hose!" yelled my brother-in-law. He opened the steel door that led to the hallway. It clanged shut behind him.

We tried to follow his voice, but we bumped into each other. We could not find our way. It was still too dark.

"Wait," I said. "If we go out in the hallway, we might get lost. And we don't know where the fire is. Let's stay here in the bedroom until we know what to do."

So we sat in the bedroom. We hoped my brother-in-law would return with a fire hose. But we heard nothing. Then the lights went out.

"Don't worry, dear," I said to Harriet. I said this even though I was shaking inside. "Let me go and see what's going on."

I swung the door open. I could not believe my eyes. Fire had swept into the living room. I felt the heat on my face. For a moment, I was in a panic. I wanted to grab Harriet and run through the flames. But even if we made it, we might not be safe. The hallway might be worse. And we didn't know our way around.

But if we stayed in the bedroom, there was no escape. We were on the fourteenth floor. There was only one window. From there, there was nowhere to go but down.

Only God could help us now. I prayed, "Lord, please help me know what to do."

Something made me go back into the bedroom. I slammed the door behind us.

Harriet saw a phone by the bed. She tried to call for help. I saw her put the phone down slowly.

"No dial tone," she said. "The phone is dead."

We heard a great crash in the living room. It seemed as if some monster were out there. Some evil force was just outside the door.

"God, please be with us," we prayed. We had no idea what to do. We thought we would never get out. But that simple prayer cleared my head. It helped me think clearly.

"Look, Harriet," I said. "God is helping us!" I pointed at the door. "That's a steel door God has given us. Flames won't burn through steel. We have to make sure it stays shut. And we need to keep the whole room good and wet. Then we may be able to keep the flames away until help comes."

Right away, we started working. Harriet and I pushed a heavy dresser in front of the door. That would keep it shut, even if the fire pushed from the other room.

There was a bathroom next to our bedroom. We turned on the faucets. Soon, the sink and the bathtub overflowed. The water soaked the rug. We also tore up towels and soaked them in the water. We put these on the vents, where smoke was coming in. I took off my shoe. Then I used my shoe to smash the window open. The cool air came in from outside.

"Help!" Harriet shouted out of the broken window. I shouted, too. But we heard no answer.

"Oh, Lord," I prayed, "what do we do now?"

I saw a plastic trash can floating in from the bathroom. "Let's use that to wet down the walls," I said. Harriet nodded.

We took turns. She would fill the trash can. I would throw the water onto the walls. We took the bedspread from the bed and soaked it. Then we tried to hang it on the wall. But it was too heavy for us. We could not lift it.

It had been an hour since we woke up. We were getting tired. Harriet lay down on the bed to rest.

"Maybe I can still save you," I told her. "We could tie the sheets end to end. Then I could lower you out the window."

Harriet shook her head. "We're on the fourteenth floor!" Then she got up from the bed with new strength. "Besides," she said, "I don't want to leave you. We will stay here. The door will keep the fire out, with God's help."

Steam was rising from the walls. We heard crashing noises from the other rooms. All around us was a burning furnace. But the steel door was keeping the fire away from us. We were thankful for it.

"Yes," I said. "You're right. We can stay here if we keep wetting down the walls. And we have to keep calling for help."

I threw a bucket of water onto the wall. It sizzled. If this room got any hotter, it would burst into flames. I saw a box on the dresser. Maybe I could throw that out the window. At least it would make someone see us.

That's what I thought. But there was only a back street beneath our window. All the people were standing in front of the building.

"No one knows we're up here," Harriet moaned. "We're lost."

I held her in my arms. By this time, I was losing hope, too. Smoke was filling the room. But we had to keep trying. "Let's keep splashing the water," I said.

Harriet nodded, and walked into the bathroom to fill the trash can. She slipped on the wet floor. I heard her cry of pain. I rushed to help.

Her ankle was broken, or at least put out of joint. It was swelling badly.

This was the last straw. Now we could not escape the flames. We had tried our best, but the fire still burned. I sat down with Harriet and grabbed a wet blanket. I wrapped the blanket around us to protect us from the heat.

We did not even talk. We just held each other. We also prayed silently. It was strange. We had come all the way to Texas so we would not be alone. And here we were, alone with each other. And that was all we really needed right now.

The fire roared like a storm. But then we heard a new sound. It was like thunder.

"It's water!" Harriet said. "Water from hoses! Firemen are putting out the fire!"

We screamed with joy. A few moments later, we heard pounding at our door. We pushed the heavy dresser aside and opened the door. We fell into the firemen's arms. They led us outside to safety.

The next day Harriet rested. She had to stay off her bad ankle. But I returned to the scene of the fire. My brother-in-law went with me.

"I went back to get you," he said. "But the fire was so bad, I thought you must have run out. Then I couldn't find you outside. So I really got worried."

A fireman led us to the fourteenth floor. The whole living room was burned black. The Christmas tree, the chairs and tables — these were all just ashes.

I looked up at the bedroom door. "That steel door," I said, "it saved our lives."

The fireman broke some black chips off the door. It wasn't steel at all. It was made of wood.

I thought back to the feelings I had the night before. Harriet and I trusted that the door would save us.

Now I know that someone else was with us. Someone far stronger than steel.

READING SCORES:
Flesch-Kincaid: 1
Gunning-Fog: 4

LITTLE BOY LOST

by Donald G. Shaffer, Somerset, Pennyslvania

The phone woke me up. I rolled over and looked at the clock. It was 3:15 A.M. Picking up the phone, I heard the voice of the town fire chief.

"Don," he said, "we have a report of a drowning. A little boy went over Swallow Falls. They need some people there to help. Can you get your scuba divers together?"

Just what I needed at three in the morning! But I was in charge of a team of scuba divers. When there were problems like this, the fire chief called us. We had to help.

I called eight other divers. We met at the fire house an hour later. We were all still sleepy.

The chief gave us the facts. A boy had been wading with his father. He was ten years old. They were in the river above Swallow Falls. All of a sudden, the current swept the boy down into the river. Then it carried him over the falls. At the bottom of the waterfall was a deep whirlpool.

The father ran down the hill beside the waterfall. He tried to dive into the whirlpool. But the water rushed too fast. It almost pulled him down, too. The father even formed a search party to search the shore. But they could not find the boy.

It sounded hopeless. I shook my head as the chief told the story. But, if it was so hopeless, why were we there?

"The boy's body has not been found," the chief said. "That means he may still be alive." We had to try to find him.

Swallow Falls was way out in the country. We drove an hour and a half to get there. Riding along, I thought about the awesome power of the falls. I had heard of other people who had drowned there. Then I thought about the boy. Could he still be alive?

I teach Sunday school at my church. I try to believe what I teach. I had taught boys about prayer, but it was hard for me to pray. I don't know why. But when I thought about those falls, I knew I would need help.

There in the truck, as we rode to the falls, I prayed. I closed my eyes and said softly, "God, help us. If that boy is still alive, give us the chance to rescue him."

When we got to Swallow Falls, the sun was coming up. We saw how tough our job would be. The waterfall was only ten feet high, but one hundred feet across. At the bottom was a raging stream. And in the stream was that whirlpool. It was swishing around like a giant funnel.

How would we ever do this? I checked out the scene as I stood on the shore. We would have to go under the falls. If the boy was still alive, he would be behind the falls. There might be hollow places in the rock. But it seemed foolish to enter the water. The water was too strong. And the current might push us into the whirlpool. That might drag us down for good.

My back-up diver, Rick, stood next to me. "Don, I'm really scared," he said. He had not been diving for very long. None of us had. I had started seven years before this. But I never had to dive into water like this.

"Rick," I said. "I'm scared, too. But we can't let our fear beat us."

First I tried to swim under the falls. I tried four times. Each time, the water pushed me back.

Then we stretched a rope across the top of the waterfall. We tied it firmly on each shore. Then we hooked a new rope around that rope, forming a T. In the stream below, I held onto this rope. That would help me keep steady as I went under the falls. Or so we thought. Again, the water bounced me around like a sponge.

We were running out of ideas.

Next, we tied a rope to a rock above the falls. I held onto this rope and tried to move through the waterfall. It worked! I found myself behind the falling water. My feet landed on a ledge of rock. But the rope caught in the rocks above me. I had to let go.

So there I was. It was like a hallway, but it was very strange. On one side the falling water formed a wall.

On the other side was a wall of rock. I was in water up to my chest. But my feet were standing on a solid ledge. The noise of the falling water filled this "hallway."

Without that rope, I had no way to get out. I wondered what the other divers thought. They would see the rope without me on the end of it. They would think that I was lost.

But now I had to try to find the boy. With the noise of the waterfall, my voice would be drowned out. So I didn't call. I just looked, as I inched my way along this ledge.

All of a sudden I looked up and saw him. The boy! He was lying on a ledge about a foot above water level. Seeing him there, I felt goose bumps.

How did he get there? The water must have swept him up onto the ledge. But the ledge was only big enough for one. It was almost as if the water had carved that ledge just for him. I was amazed. *God's hand must have placed him there,* I thought.

I moved closer to the boy. His eyes were closed, but he was alive. I worried about what would happen if he opened his eyes just then. He would see me in my scuba gear. I must have looked like some monster. And this place was spooky enough!

The boy saw me and sat up. He was scared. I worked my way over to him. "Are you all right?" I asked, putting my arm around him.

"Yes," he said. His blue eyes glowed brightly, but he seemed calm now.

Now what? I was here with him. But now we were both trapped.

"Let's do this," I said. "Let's ask God to get us out of here."

The boy was eager to do this. He turned over and folded his hands. Then he bowed his head. I did the same.

"Dear God," I said. "Please help us to get out of this alive."

Now, how were we going to do this? First, I thought we might "buddy-breathe." That is, we would take turns breathing through my scuba gear. But that seemed too hard to do.

I decided to use the scuba gear myself. I would hold the boy in my arms and try to dive out. The boy might swallow some water, but not much. So I hoped.

Taking the boy in my arms, I inched back along the ledge. I was looking for a place where the water was weaker. But the water was falling with full force. Every so often, a sheet of water would fall on us. But the boy remained calm.

Then the ledge dropped off. My scuba tank got stuck in the rock. We couldn't move sideways now. We had to dive forward, through the full force of the waterfall.

I looked at the boy. He was still calm. I pointed to the wall of water. "We're going to have to swim through that," I said. "Take a deep breath."

"OK," he said. I was amazed by his courage. The boy swung around to face me. He locked his arms around my neck, his legs around my waist. With all my power, I pushed off with my legs into the water.

The waterfall drove us down, down, down into a swirling darkness. For about fifteen seconds, we were tossed around. Then I began to kick my flippers wildly. It was a race against time. I had to get the boy's head above water.

I grabbed the boy by the waist. Using every bit of my strength, I threw him upward. I was glad for all the years I had worked with concrete blocks. That work had built strength in my arms. Now I could use that to save a life.

As the boy shot up past me, my breathing gear came loose. I began to swallow water. But now I was rising to the surface, too.

When my head broke the surface of the water, I heard yelling. A diver was diving in from the shore to grab the boy. We had made it! We had missed the whirlpool by inches!

Soon a rowboat was by my side. I grabbed onto it. I was very tired, but very happy.

Later, the boy's father called me. He thanked me for saving his son's life. I learned that the boy's name was Richard. I was able to visit Richard months later. He's a swell little guy who loves baseball. Believe it or not, he also loves swimming.

Neither of us will ever forget that day at the falls.
God heard our prayers that day. He gave us the
courage to find our way out.

READING SCORES:
Flesch-Kincaid: 1
Gunning-Fog: 4

CHRISTMAS GIFTS
by Diane Rayner, Bellevue, Washington

Christmas is a time when strange and lovely things happen. I have always believed that. It's a time when wise men visit babies. It's a time when babies are born in feed bins. It's a time when special stars light the sky. Of course, it's the time when God came to us as a little child.

And so Christmas has always held a special magic for me. It became even more special one year. That was when my son Marty was eight.

My three children and I had moved into a trailer that year. We lived in a woodsy area. As Christmas came near, we were happy. Even though the weather was often rainy, our spirits stayed high.

Marty seemed brighter than any of us. He was the youngest, blonde-haired and playful. He had a cute way of looking at you. He would tilt his head like a puppy. This was really because he was deaf in one ear. But he did not seem to mind.

All month, Marty was very busy. Something was going on. He made his bed each day. He set the table for dinner. He even helped his brother and sister make the meal. I paid him a small amount each week for these chores. But he would not spend this money. He was saving it up. I did not know why. But I thought it might have something to do with Kenny.

Kenny was Marty's friend. They had met in the spring. Since then, you could not tear them apart. If you called one, you got both. They played with each other in a nearby field. They caught frogs and snakes in the stream. They dug for hidden treasure. They fed peanuts to the squirrels.

Times were hard for the kids and me. We had to be careful with our money. I worked as a meat wrapper. My pay helped us get by. But we didn't have much.

Yet it was even harder for Kenny's mother. She was trying to raise her two kids on even less money. They were very poor. But they were proud. Kenny's mother had strict rules. She raised her children well.

We worked all month to get ready for Christmas. We made pretty things to hang on the tree. And we made gifts for each other.

Sometimes Marty and Kenny would sit still long enough to make something. A basket, maybe, or a horn of plenty. But then, in a flash, they would be gone. Out the door. They would slide under the charged fence and out into their field. We had that fence for safety. Just in case any man or beast tried to sneak in. The fence would send a shock, and send them away. But

Marty and Kenny had no problem with the fence. They would slide under it in a second.

A few nights before Christmas, Marty came to me. I was making cookies. "Mom," he said, "I bought Kenny a present. Want to see it?"

So that's what he's been up to, I thought.

"It's something Kenny has wanted for a long, long time," Marty said. He wiped his hands on a dish towel. Then he pulled a box out of his pocket.

I took the box and lifted the lid. It was a compass. Marty had saved his money to buy a compass for his friend. Now they could wander in the woods like Lewis and Clark.

"It's a lovely gift, Martin," I said. But then I thought about Kenny's mother. They were so poor. Kenny would not be able to give a gift to Marty. And Kenny's mother would not let him take a gift without giving one.

I tried to tell this to Marty. He knew what I was saying. "I know, Mom. I know! But what if it was a secret? What if they never knew who gave it?"

I didn't know how to answer him. I just did not know.

The day before Christmas was rainy and gray. We were all busy getting our home ready. It kept raining into the night. In an odd way, I felt sad as I looked out the window. It was such a dull day outside. I could not picture wise men riding through this weather. Could any strange and lovely thing happen today? I doubted it.

I turned from the window. I checked the food I was making for our Christmas feast. Then I saw Marty slip out the door. He wore his coat over his bed clothes. And he held a tiny, nicely wrapped box in his pocket.

He ran across the wet field. He slipped under the charged fence. He rushed across the yard to Kenny's house. He climbed the steps on tiptoe. He opened the screen door just a crack. He put the box on the doorstep. He reached for the doorbell. He pressed it hard.

Then Marty turned and ran. Down the steps. Across the yard. All of a sudden, he ran into the fence.

The shock knocked him down. He lay on the ground, stunned. He gasped for breath. Then he slowly stood up. Weakly, he walked back home.

"Marty," I said when I saw him. "What happened?" He had tears in his eyes. His lower lip shook.

"I forgot about the fence," he said. "It knocked me down."

I hugged his muddy little body. He was still in a daze. There was a red line on his face. It ran from his mouth to his ear. That was where he hit the fence. It looked badly burned. I began to treat it. Then I got Marty a hot drink and put him to bed.

As I tucked him in, Marty looked up at me. "Mom," he said. "Kenny didn't see me. I'm sure he didn't see me."

That night I was puzzled. I was sad. It seemed wrong for God to let this happen. This little boy was doing a lovely thing. He was giving a gift to his friend. And in secret, too. Surely that's the kind of thing God wants us all to do. I did not sleep well that night. Christmas had lost its magic. There seemed to be nothing special about it anymore.

I was wrong.

In the morning, the sun was shining. Marty still had that red line on his face. But the burn was not very bad. We opened our presents. Then Kenny showed up. He was eager to show Marty his new compass. He had no idea who gave it to him. Marty just smiled and smiled.

Then I saw something. As the two boys talked, Marty was not tilting his head. He seemed to be hearing with his bad ear.

A few weeks later we got the report from the school nurse. "Marty now has full hearing in both ears."

We don't know how it happened. Doctors think that the shock from the fence did it. Maybe so. It just seems to me that Marty got a Christmas gift from the Lord. He was giving a gift in secret. God was giving something in return.

So Christmas still has its magic. Strange and lovely things do happen on this night. No matter what the weather is.

WORD LIST

a *408*
A.M. *1*
able *6*
about *67*
above *6*
accept *1*
ached *2*
acres *1*
across *11*
added *1*
admit *1*
adult *2*
afloat *1*
afraid *17*
after *10*
again *38*
against *12*
age *5*
ago *3*
ahead *6*
air *3*
airplane *2*
airplanes *1*
airport *7*
alert *3*
alive *15*
all *91*
almighty *1*
almost *8*
alone *7*
along *10*
also *11*
always *13*
am *22*
amazed *2*
amazing *1*
amount *1*
an *14*
and *241*
anger *1*
angry *4*

ankle *2*
another *1*
answer *6*
answered *7*
answers *1*
any *20*
anyone *2*
apart *4*
are *30*
area *6*
aren't *1*
arm *6*
arms *23*
around *46*
arrest *2*
as *62*
ashes *1*
aside *1*
ask *8*
asked *23*
asking *2*
asleep *2*
at *102*
ate *4*
awake *2*
awards *1*
away *38*
awesome *1*
awful *3*

babies *2*
baby *4*
baby-sitters *1*
baby-sitting *1*
back *63*
back-up *3*
backed *1*
backing *1*
backwards *1*
bad *18*
badly *7*

bag *3*
bags *1*
banged *1*
bank *2*
baptist *1*
bar *3*
barb *10*
barely *1*
baseball *1*
basement *2*
basket *1*
bathroom *3*
bathtub *1*
baton *1*
be *74*
heard *1*
beast *1*
beat *2*
beating *2*
became *4*
because *4*
bed *18*
bedroom *9*
bedspread *1*
been *32*
before *24*
began *18*
beginning *1*
behind *13*
being *3*
believe *8*
believed *1*
below *2*
bend *2*
beneath *1*
bent *4*
beside *2*
best *8*
bet *3*
better *13*
Betty *4*

Bible *12*
big *5*
bigger *2*
Bill *15*
hills *1*
bins *1*
bit *5*
bits *1*
bitter *2*
black *2*
blackness *2*
blame *1*
blank *1*
blanket *5*
blankets *1*
blast *1*
bleach *1*
bleeding *3*
blessings *1*
blew *3*
blind *1*
blindfold *6*
blocks *2*
blonde-haired *2*
blood *2*
bloody *1*
blowing *3*
blown *2*
blue *1*
blue-collar *1*
blue-eyed *1*
boat *4*
body *8*
bomb *8*
bombs *5*
bone *1*
book *8*
bored *1*
boring *4*
born *1*
boss *1*

bosses *1*
both *10*
bothered *3*
bothers *1*
bottom *8*
bought *1*
bounced *3*
bowed *1*
box *7*
boxes *3*
boy *27*
boy's *4*
boys *3*
brace *2*
braces *3*
brakes *1*
break *1*
breakfast *2*
breaking *3*
breath *7*
breathe *1*
breathing *4*
bricks *3*
bridge *11*
bright *1*
brighter *1*
brightly *1*
bring *1*
broke *10*
broken *7*
Bronx *1*
Brooklyn *1*
brother *2*
brother-in-law *3*
brought *7*
brown-haired *1*
bruises *1*
brushed *1*
bucket *1*
buckner *1*
buddy *1*

buddy-breathe *1*
building *13*
buildings *1*
built *3*
bulbs *1*
bumped *2*
bumper *1*
bumps *1*
bun *1*
bundled *1*
burglars *1*
burn *4*
burned *4*
burning *3*
burst *3*
busy *2*
but *197*
button *1*
buy *1*
buzzed *1*
by *38*

cab *1*
cafe *1*
call *9*
called *17*
calling *2*
calls *2*
calm *7*
calmly *1*
came *49*
camp *2*
can *38*
can't *9*
car *62*
care *5*
cared *5*
career *1*
careful *4*
cares *1*
Carole *4*
Carolina *1*
carried *1*
carry *2*
cars *8*
carved *1*
case *5*
catch *6*
Cathy *2*

caught *11*
ceiling *1*
center *1*
certain *1*
chairs *1*
chance *2*
change *2*
changed *5*
changes *1*
charge *2*
charged *2*
Charlotte *1*
check *2*
checked *4*
cheek *1*
cheer *2*
cheered *1*
cheerful *1*
chest *3*
chicken *2*
chief *5*
chiefs *1*
child *5*
children *11*
chips *1*
choice *2*
choked *1*
choose *1*
chores *2*
Christ *2*
Christian *2*
Christians *1*
Christmas *16*
church *8*
city *2*
clanged *1*
class *1*
clean-cut *1*
clear *3*
cleared *3*
clearer *1*
clearly *2*
climb *3*
climbed *3*
clock *1*
close *10*
closed *6*
closer *2*
closing *1*

clothes *2*
clouds *5*
club *2*
coat *4*
coffee *2*
cold *8*
college *2*
come *15*
comes *1*
coming *7*
common *2*
compared *1*
compass *3*
concrete *1*
confused *1*
control *1*
controlled *1*
controls *1*
cook *1*
cookies *1*
cool *3*
cop *5*
cop-and-
robber *1*
cops *5*
corner *2*
corners *1*
coughing *1*
could *79*
couldn't *12*
counting *1*
country *1*
couple *3*
courage *4*
course *3*
cousin *2*
covered *3*
crack *1*
cracked *1*
cramps *1*
crash *12*
crashed *3*
crashing *1*
crawled *2*
crazy *5*
creams *1*
credit *1*
creepy *1*
cried *4*

cries *1*
cross *2*
crossing *2*
crowd *2*
crowds *1*
crushed *2*
cry *1*
crying *3*
cure *1*
curled *1*
current *2*
cut *2*
cute *1*
cuts *1*

dad *10*
daddy *1*
dairy *1*
Dallas *2*
dam *8*
danger *5*
dangers *1*
Daniel *1*
Dansville *1*
dark *10*
darkness *3*
dashboard *1*
daughter *1*
Dave *1*
Davis *1*
dawn *4*
day *31*
days *5*
daze *2*
dead *5*
deaf *1*
deal *2*
dean *1*
dear *7*
death *7*
decided *2*
deep *4*
deeply *1*
delight *1*
den *1*
dial *1*
dialed *1*
Diane *1*
did *40*

didn't *32*
die *8*
died *5*
dinner *5*
dirt *1*
dish *1*
distance *1*
dive *4*
diver *2*
divers *4*
diving *2*
Dixie *1*
dizzy *1*
do *52*
doctor *3*
doctors *9*
does *1*
doesn't *1*
dog *3*
doing *4*
dollars *1*
don *8*
don't *31*
Donald *1*
done *7*
Donnie *1*
door *38*
doorbell *2*
doors *1*
doorstep *1*
dorm *1*
double-crossed *1*
doubted *1*
doubts *7*
down *54*
downtown *1*
drag *1*
dragged *1*
dreams *2*
dress *2*
dresser *3*
drew *1*
drink *2*
drive *2*
driver *5*
driveway *1*
driving *8*
drop *6*
dropped *8*

dropping *1*
drove *7*
drowned *2*
drowning *1*
drug *1*
drugs *2*
drum *1*
drunk *1*
dry *3*
dug *1*
dull *2*
dusty *1*
duty *1*
dwell *1*
dwelling *1*
dying *1*

each *29*
eager *3*
ear *7*
early *2*
earn *1*
ears *2*
earth *2*
east *1*
easy *3*
eat *2*
eaten *1*
eating *1*
eby *1*
Ecuador *2*
egg *1*
eggs *1*
eight *3*
eighteen *1*
eighteen-
  wheeler *1*
eighty *1*
either *1*
else *13*
empty *4*
end *4*
engine *1*
enjoyed *2*
enough *11*
enter *1*
entered *1*
escape *2*
Eunice *2*

eve *2*
even *31*
evening *1*
ever *4*
every *4*
everybody *1*
everyone *1*
evil *1*
expect *1*
explain *1*
explode *3*
extra *1*
eye *4*
eyes *16*

face *6*
faces *1*
facing *3*
facts *1*
faith *19*
fall *4*
fallen *1*
falling *9*
falls *17*
family *2*
fancy *1*
far *4*
fast *9*
father *14*
father's *2*
faucets *1*
fault *1*
FBI *1*
fear *7*
fears *1*
feast *1*
fed *1*
feed *1*
feel *20*
feeling *12*
feelings *2*
feet *16*
fell *14*
felt *30*
fence *9*
few *20*
field *3*
fifteen *1*
fifty *3*

fifty-five *1*
fifty-two *1*
fight *3*
figure *1*
figured *2*
fill *2*
filled *1*
filling *2*
find *14*
fine *7*
finger *1*
fingers *4*
fire *47*
fired *1*
fireman *2*
firemen *1*
firemen's *1*
firmly *1*
first *20*
fit *1*
five *10*
five-foot-four *1*
five-foot-ten *1*
fix *2*
fixing *2*
flag *3*
flames *7*
flash *4*
flashing *1*
flashlight *3*
flew *2*
flight *1*
flipped *1*
flippers *1*
float *1*
floated *1*
floating *4*
flood *1*
floor *13*
flow *1*
flowed *1*
flu *2*
fly *7*
flying *3*
fog *1*
folded *2*
follow *1*
food *1*
fool *1*

foolish *1*
foot *3*
for *121*
force *4*
forced *2*
forests *1*
forget *3*
forgive *1*
forgives *1*
forgot *2*
formed *2*
forming *1*
fort *2*
forty-foot *1*
forty-two *1*
forward *5*
fought *2*
found *8*
four *4*
four-story *1*
fourteen *4*
Frank *13*
flee *1*
freeze *1*
Friday *2*
friend *6*
friends *6*
frightened *2*
frogs *1*
from *50*
front *11*
fry *1*
full *6*
funnel *1*
funny *1*
furnace *1*

gallons *1*
game *1*
gap *1*
garage *4*
garbage *1*
gas *4*
gasped *2*
gate *2*
gatepost *1*
gates *3*
gather *2*
gathered *1*

gave *19*
gear *5*
gentle *1*
gently *1*
george *1*
Georgia *1*
German *1*
get *55*
getting *4*
giant *2*
gift *6*
gifts *2*
girl *3*
girlfriend *2*
girls *7*
give *17*
given *3*
gives *1*
giving *5*
glad *5*
glass *6*
glasses *1*
glory *2*
glove *1*
glow *1*
glowed *1*
go *36*
goal *1*
God *123*
God's *7*
going *28*
gold *1*
gone *13*
good *20*
goose *1*
got *51*
gotten *2*
grab *3*
grabbed *10*
gray *4*
great *7*
grew *1*
gripped *1*
ground *5*
groups *1*
grow *1*
growing *1*
grown *1*
guard *3*

guarded 2
guess 3
guest 1
guide 1
gun 5
gunshot 1
gut 2
guts 2
guy 6
guys 4

habit 2
had 188
hadn't 2
hair 1
half 3
hall 1
hallway 5
hallway 1
hand 5
handcuffs 1
handed 1
handle 3
hands 5
hang 3
hanging 1
happen 12
happened 11
happy 8
hard 14
harder 1
hardest 1
hardly 3
Harriet 17
has 14
hat 3
haul 2
hauling 1
have 63
haven't 1
he 254
he'd 1
he'll 1
he's 4
head 21
headed 3
headlight 1
healed 1
health 1

hear 9
heard 37
hearing 5
heart 4
heat 3
heavy 7
held 14
help 54
helped 18
helpful 1
helping 4
helpless 1
her 43
here 24
hero 3
hey 3
hidden 2
hide 1
hiding 2
high 6
higher 1
highway 4
hill 8
him 69
himself 2
his 85
hit 9
hold 2
holding 3
hole 1
hollow 1
home 26
homes 1
honked 1
honking 1
hood 2
hooked 1
hope 3
hoped 2
hopeless 2
horn 2
hose 2
hoses 1
hot 3
hotter 1
hour 4
hour-and-
   a-half 1
hours 4

house 12
how 35
huddle 1
huddled 1
huge 3
hugged 2
hundred 3
hung 2
hunger 1
hunk 1
hurried 2
hurry 3
hurt 24
hurting 1
husband 14
husband's 1
husbands 1
hymn 1
hymns 2

I 1,124
I'd 1
I'll 5
I'm 22
I've 3
ice 2
icy 2
idea 3
ideas 2
if 50
Illinois 1
in 219
inched 2
inches 2
Indiana 1
Indianapolis 1
inside 14
insides 1
instead 2
into 55
is 66
Isaiah 3
isn't 2
it 275
it's 13
its 6

jail 3
jammed 4

jaw 1
Jell-O 1
Jeremy 14
Jeremy's 1
Jerry 16
Jess 5
Jesse 17
Jesse's 1
Jesus 5
job 14
jobs 1
John's 1
Johnson 3
join 2
joined 1
joint 1
joke 4
jolt 1
Jose 3
joy 3
Joyce 3
judge 2
juice 1
julio 2
jump 4
jumped 5
junk 2
just 58

keep 20
keeping 3
keeps 1
Kelly 4
Kelly's 1
Kenny 9
Kenny's 5
kept 18
Kevin 4
Kevin's 1
kick 1
kicked 2
kid 1
kidded 2
kidding 1
kidnap 1
kidnapped 1
kids 25
kill 4
killed 5

Kim 8
Kim's 1
kind 3
kissed 1
kitchen 1
knelt 1
knew 27
knock 1
knocked 3
know 44
knows 3

ladder 1
lady 3
lake 2
lakes 1
land 5
landed 4
lane 2
lanes 1
large 2
larger 1
last 7
late 7
later 16
laugh 2
laughed 2
laughing 1
lay 5
leading 2
leaned 1
learn 2
learned 12
learning 3
least 8
leave 4
led 7
ledge 10
left 14
legs 8
less 2
lesson 2
lessons 1
let 28
let's 8
letting 3
level 1
Lewis 1
lid 2

life *21*	lying *5*	middle *2*	narrow *1*	often *2*
lifelines *2*		might *25*	Nate *6*	oh *7*
lift *2*	mad *4*	mile *1*	Nate's *1*	OK *6*
lifted *2*	made *33*	miles *4*	near *5*	old *9*
lifting *1*	magic *3*	million *3*	nearby *1*	oldest *1*
light *6*	magnet *1*	mind *11*	nearly *2*	on *125*
lights *5*	mail *1*	mine *4*	neck *8*	once *7*
like *42*	major *1*	Minnesota *1*	need *8*	one *65*
liked *2*	make *17*	minute *3*	needed *9*	one's *1*
limit *1*	makes *3*	minutes *9*	needy *1*	ones *4*
Linda *2*	making *3*	mirror *3*	neighbors *1*	only *34*
line *5*	man *27*	miss *2*	neither *1*	onto *15*
lino *1*	man's *1*	missed *2*	nerves *1*	open *12*
lions *1*	man-made *1*	mission *5*	never *20*	opened *14*
lip *1*	many *7*	mistake *1*	new *30*	or *15*
list *2*	march *1*	moaned *2*	news *1*	orange *2*
listen *2*	marriage *2*	mom *3*	next *16*	order *2*
lit *1*	married *3*	moment *6*	nice *1*	other *53*
little *16*	Martin *1*	moments *3*	nicely *1*	other's *2*
live *11*	Marty *20*	Monday *1*	night *19*	others *13*
lived *8*	Marty's *1*	money *14*	nights *1*	our *37*
lives *1*	Mary *5*	monster *3*	no *43*	ourselves *2*
living *9*	mask *1*	month *3*	nodded *5*	out *94*
load *5*	masks *1*	months *7*	noise *4*	outside *17*
locked *1*	master *1*	mood *2*	noises *2*	over *40*
long *7*	matches *1*	more *16*	none *1*	overflowed *1*
longer *1*	matter *1*	morning *9*	noon *2*	own *6*
look *11*	Matthew *1*	most *4*	normal *1*	
looked *41*	may *5*	motel *3*	Norman *1*	pacing *1*
looking *9*	maybe *12*	mother *7*	north *1*	paddle *1*
loose *4*	me *288*	mountain *3*	nose *1*	pages *2*
Lord *30*	meal *1*	mountains *1*	not *96*	paid *1*
Lord's *1*	mean *1*	mouth *3*	note *1*	pain *8*
lose *2*	meaning *1*	move *16*	nothing *6*	pains *1*
losing *1*	means *2*	moved *12*	notice *1*	panic *1*
loss *2*	meant *1*	moving *5*	now *69*	paper *1*
lost *13*	meat *1*	much *13*	nowhere *3*	parents *11*
lot *4*	medics *4*	muddy *2*	numb *1*	parked *4*
lots *3*	meet *1*	mumbled *1*	number *1*	part *2*
loud *1*	men *19*	music *2*	nurse *4*	partner *5*
louder *1*	mental *1*	must *9*	nurse's *1*	partner's *1*
love *2*	mercy *2*	my *308*	nurses *3*	party *1*
lovely *11*	merry-go-	myself *25*		pass *4*
loves *4*	round *1*		o'clock *5*	passed *3*
loving *1*	mess *2*	nabbed *1*	Oakland *2*	past *1*
low *1*	message *1*	nagging *2*	odd *1*	pastor *1*
lower *2*	met *5*	name *5*	of *239*	patch *1*
lunch *1*	metal *7*	named *3*	off *32*	patients *1*
lungs *3*	Mexico *1*	Nancy *1*	office *1*	Paul *3*

pay *3*	poor *4*	quits *1*	return *2*	safety *3*
peace *2*	pop *2*	quitter *2*	returned *1*	said *149*
peanuts *1*	Portland *1*	quitting *2*	Richard *3*	sake *1*
peeked *1*	pounding *3*	race *1*	Rick *1*	sales *2*
penny *1*	pounds *5*	raced *2*	rid *1*	same *4*
Pennyslvania *1*	power *5*	radio *7*	ride *3*	sandwich *1*
people *37*	pranks *3*	radios *1*	riding *2*	sang *1*
people's *1*	pray *5*	raging *1*	rig *1*	sank *1*
perfect *2*	prayed *31*	rail *3*	right *37*	sat *12*
perish *2*	prayer *11*	railroad *1*	right-handed *1*	Saturday *1*
person *4*	prayers *1*	rain *6*	ripped *3*	save *10*
Peterson *1*	praying *9*	rain's *1*	risen *1*	saved *4*
Philippians *1*	present *1*	rainbow *1*	rising *2*	saving *2*
phone *10*	presents *1*	raining *5*	river *9*	saw *40*
pick *5*	president *1*	rainy *2*	road *8*	say *14*
picked *2*	pressed *2*	raise *7*	roads *1*	saying *7*
picking *1*	pretend *3*	raised *2*	roar *1*	says *3*
picture *5*	pretty *3*	raising *1*	roared *3*	scared *11*
pictures *1*	prison *1*	rammed *1*	roaring *1*	scarf *1*
piece *3*	probably *1*	ran *14*	robber *2*	scary *7*
pieces *2*	problem *1*	rang *1*	Robert *2*	scene *6*
pile *1*	problems *4*	ransom *1*	rock *5*	school *4*
pillars *1*	products *5*	rather *1*	rocks *1*	scores *2*
pilot *7*	protect *2*	ray *18*	rode *1*	scrape *1*
pilot's *1*	protecting *1*	reach *2*	roll *1*	scratch *1*
pilots *1*	proud *1*	reached *9*	rolled *1*	scream *1*
pinned *3*	prove *1*	reaching *1*	Romans *1*	screamed *4*
pity *1*	Psalms *2*	read *3*	Ron *4*	screaming *2*
place *13*	pull *2*	reading *3*	Ronald *1*	screeched *1*
placed *1*	pulled *17*	ready *4*	roof *5*	screeching *1*
places *4*	pumped *1*	Reagan *1*	rookie *1*	screen *1*
plan *3*	punch *1*	real *10*	room *30*	scuba *6*
plane *10*	punched *1*	really *11*	rooms *1*	search *2*
planes *1*	punching *1*	red *4*	rope *9*	searle *1*
planned *2*	puppy *1*	reeled *1*	rough *1*	seat *8*
planning *2*	pure *1*	refuge *1*	rowboat *1*	second *3*
plans *1*	push *1*	relax *3*	rubbed *1*	seconds *3*
plastic *3*	pushed *14*	relaxed *1*	rug *4*	secret *3*
play *1*	put *21*	relief *1*	rules *1*	see *32*
played *1*	puts *1*	remained *1*	run *7*	seeing *1*
playful *1*	putting *3*	remember *1*	runners *1*	seem *3*
playing *1*	puzzled *1*	reminds *1*	running *7*	seemed *16*
plays *1*		report *6*	runway *1*	seems *1*
please *16*	queen *1*	reports *1*	rushed *8*	self-pity *1*
plenty *1*	question *1*	rescue *3*		self-support *1*
pocket *2*	questions *3*	rescued *2*	sad *6*	sell *3*
pointed *8*	quickly *2*	resist *1*	sadness *1*	selling *4*
pointing *3*	quiet *4*	rest *8*	safe *15*	send *4*
police *16*	quit *1*	rested *1*	safely *2*	sending *1*

sends *1*	side *18*	smoke *9*	spot *1*	straw *1*
sense *3*	sides *2*	snack *1*	spreading *3*	stream *4*
sensed *1*	sidewalk *2*	snakes *1*	spring *1*	street *11*
senses *1*	sideways *2*	snapped *3*	spun *1*	strength *9*
sent *3*	sighed *1*	sneak *2*	squad *2*	stretched *2*
serve *3*	sight *4*	sniff *1*	squeeze *3*	strict *1*
service *1*	sign *1*	snow *1*	squeezed *2*	strong *8*
set *5*	signal *1*	so *55*	squirrels *1*	stronger *3*
settle *2*	silent *2*	soaked *3*	stabbed *1*	stuck *5*
seven *2*	silently *1*	soaps *1*	stairs *1*	student *1*
seventy-five *1*	silly *2*	soda *2*	stale *1*	students *2*
Sgt. *1*	simple *1*	softly *4*	stand *2*	stumble *1*
shack *1*	since *9*	solid *2*	standing *3*	stumps *1*
shadows *1*	sing *4*	some *32*	Stanley *6*	stunned *2*
shag *2*	sink *1*	someone *20*	stars *1*	suburbs *1*
shaken *1*	sinking *2*	Somerset *1*	start *3*	such *1*
shaking *4*	sins *1*	something *32*	started *11*	sudden *17*
shame *1*	sister *6*	sometimes *9*	starting *4*	suffer *1*
shape *4*	sit *5*	somewhere *1*	state *1*	sun *3*
share *1*	six *4*	son *2*	states *1*	Sunday *3*
she *55*	six-foot-two *2*	son's *1*	station *2*	sung *2*
she'll *1*	sixth *1*	sons *2*	stay *12*	sunset *1*
sheet *1*	sixty *1*	soon *17*	stayed *4*	supper *2*
sheets *1*	sizzled *1*	sore *1*	stays *1*	supplies *4*
shining *2*	ski *1*	sorry *4*	steady *2*	supposed *2*
shirt *2*	skid *1*	sound *8*	stealing *1*	sure *9*
shivered *3*	skies *1*	sounded *3*	steam *1*	surely *3*
shock *5*	skill *1*	soundly *1*	steel *9*	surface *3*
shoe *2*	sky *4*	south *4*	steering *2*	surprise *1*
shook *7*	slammed *2*	Spanish *6*	step *1*	suspect *1*
shoot *4*	sleep *1*	spare *1*	stepped *2*	swallow *6*
shoots *1*	sleeping *4*	speak *1*	steps *4*	swayed *1*
shopping *2*	sleepy *1*	speaker *1*	Steve *9*	swell *1*
shore *4*	slept *1*	speaking *1*	sticks *2*	swelling *1*
short *4*	slid *2*	special *7*	stiff *2*	swept *4*
shot *3*	slide *3*	spend *5*	still *56*	swim *3*
shotgun *5*	sliding *2*	spending *1*	stomach *1*	swimming *1*
should *14*	slip *2*	spent *1*	stood *10*	swirling *1*
shoulder *1*	slipped *3*	spider *2*	stop *5*	swishing *1*
shoulders *2*	slot *1*	spiders *1*	stopped *21*	switch *1*
shouldn't *1*	slow *3*	spilling *1*	stopping *1*	swung *2*
shout *2*	slowly *7*	spin *1*	store *2*	
shouted *15*	slump *1*	spinning *1*	storm *3*	table *1*
shouting *1*	small *13*	spirits *1*	story *9*	tables *1*
show *5*	smash *4*	splashing *1*	straight *3*	take *21*
showed *4*	smashed *5*	splendor *2*	strange *14*	taken *2*
showers *1*	smashing *1*	spoke *2*	strangers *1*	taking *4*
shut *4*	smell *2*	sponge *1*	strap *1*	talk *16*
sick *7*	smiled *5*	spooky *1*	strapped *1*	talked *12*

talking *10*	threw *4*	train *9*	use *5*	we'll *2*
tall *2*	thrill *1*	trained *1*	used *9*	we're *5*
tank *2*	throat *1*	trapped *6*	useless *1*	we've *1*
tanks *2*	through *38*	trash *3*	using *1*	weak *1*
tasted *1*	throw *2*	treasure *1*		weaker *2*
taught *6*	thrown *4*	treat *1*	vain *1*	weakly *1*
teach *4*	thud *1*	tree *3*	values *1*	wear *1*
teacher *2*	thunder *3*	trees *2*	vents *1*	weather *8*
teaching *1*	ticked *2*	tried *36*	verse *6*	week *3*
team *1*	tie *3*	trigger *2*	very *36*	weekend *1*
tear *1*	tied *5*	trimming *1*	viewing *1*	weeks *3*
tears *4*	tight *2*	trouble *3*	village *4*	weight *1*
tell *8*	tilt *1*	troubled *2*	villages *1*	well *10*
telling *5*	tilting *1*	truck *22*	visit *2*	went *46*
tells *2*	time *33*	trucker *2*	visits *1*	were *123*
tempted *1*	times *7*	truckers *1*	voice *18*	weren't *1*
ten *8*	tiny *2*	trucks *7*		wet *5*
tense *1*	tip *1*	true *2*	wading *1*	wetting *1*
Texas *6*	tiptoe *1*	trunk *2*	waist *2*	what *57*
than *7*	tire *1*	trust *8*	wait *3*	what's *2*
thank *12*	tired *6*	trusted *4*	waited *1*	wheel *3*
thanked *3*	tires *1*	trusting *2*	waiting *3*	wheelchair *2*
thankful *1*	to *568*	truth *1*	wake *1*	when *40*
that *169*	Toccoa *3*	try *13*	walk *16*	where *14*
that's *16*	today *4*	trying *9*	walked *10*	which *1*
the *948*	together *2*	tucked *1*	walking *2*	while *1*
their *17*	told *25*	turned *14*	wall *10*	whirlpool *5*
them *39*	tone *1*	turning *2*	walls *5*	whistle *3*
themselves *1*	tonight *1*	turns *2*	wander *1*	white *1*
then *124*	tons *3*	twenty *2*	wandered *1*	who *25*
there *90*	Tony *8*	twenty-eight *1*	want *24*	who's *1*
there's *2*	too *39*	twisted *2*	wanted *13*	whole *9*
these *15*	took *21*	twister *2*	wants *4*	why *10*
they *106*	tools *2*	twisting *1*	war *2*	wide *1*
they'll *1*	top *6*	twitched *1*	ward *1*	wife *7*
thick *1*	tore *1*	two *31*	warm *1*	wife's *1*
thicker *1*	tossed *1*		was *535*	wiggling *1*
thing *12*	touched *4*	ugly *1*	Washington *1*	wildly *1*
things *23*	tough *3*	under *14*	wasn't *7*	will *31*
think *17*	tow *1*	unfair *1*	waste *1*	wind *3*
thinking *6*	toward *9*	unload *1*	watch *3*	window *20*
thirty *2*	towel *1*	unstrap *1*	watching *2*	windows *3*
thirty-five *1*	towels *1*	until *7*	water *51*	windshield *4*
this *81*	towered *1*	up *83*	waterfall *10*	winter *1*
those *19*	town *6*	upset *4*	Watson *8*	wiped *1*
though *2*	tracks *3*	upstairs *1*	waved *2*	wise *2*
thought *73*	traffic *1*	uptight *1*	waving *1*	wish *3*
thoughts *2*	trail *1*	upward *1*	way *32*	with *91*
three *12*	trailer *1*	us *79*	we *257*	without *5*

wives *1*	wore *2*	would *93*	yards *4*	you're *8*
woke *4*	work *17*	wouldn't *3*	yeah *1*	you've *1*
woman *21*	worked *8*	wrapped *3*	year *4*	young *4*
woman's *2*	worker *2*	wrapper *1*	year's *1*	youngest *1*
won *1*	workers *3*	wrists *1*	years *15*	your *13*
won't *5*	working *4*	write *4*	yelled *5*	yourself *2*
wondered *4*	works *1*	wrong *4*	yelling *1*	
wood *2*	world *1*	wrote *2*	yellow *1*	zoomed *1*
wooden *1*	worried *3*		yes *4*	
woods *1*	worry *4*	x-ray *1*	yet *3*	
woodsy *1*	worse *8*		York *7*	
word *3*	worship *2*	yank *1*	you *141*	
words *7*	worth *2*	yard *2*	you'll *3*